How to Use Your
Creative Spirit to
Manage Depression

A Joyful Life

MICHÈLE SWIDERSKI

KiCam
PROJECTS

Cover and book design by Mark Sullivan
Author photo: Robert Preidt

ISBN 978-0-9977222-1-5

Published by KiCam Projects
www.KiCamProjects.com

Printed in the United States of America.
Printed on acid-free paper.

CONTENTS

For Robert, who stood quietly by my side from the start and supported me through life-changing decisions. Thank you for saying the things that need saying, even when difficult for me to hear. Thank you for being my writing coach, photographer, and friendly first editor— I trust you completely. You are the best!

I have always been fascinated by seeing buildings imploded, especially those tall ones coming down on a busy city street like we sometimes see on the news. It's impressive. How deafening the sound must be. My imagination is captured by the wonder of the scene, by the expert engineering and intricate planning needed to accomplish such a project while ensuring that the streetscape surrounding the building remains intact as if the neighboring structures had no idea what just happened.

Forcing a skyscraper to crumble at one person's command takes months of sophisticated planning and preparation from a variety of experts, all for something that lasts only a few seconds. And knowing that no two implosions can ever be executed in exactly the same way fascinates me. There's something pure about it, to decimate a giant structure with the least amount of external disruption.

Now, imagine if your brain experienced such an implosion. Not as a result of a well-orchestrated plan but from having abdicated its responsibility for managing the chemistry in your synapses, the ones that control your thoughts and behaviors. In what might seem like a few seconds, the mind just checks out. Poof! I am outta here! It's not that your mind is otherwise occupied by a daydream or is busy with meditation. It is simply vacant, not on call anymore. Why would your mind want to do this?

In my case, my mind checked out in an attempt at self-preservation. It no longer could cope with the demands of life and the expectations I had placed on myself. At a subconscious level, it was all too much. Rather than my brain cracking in a visible and public way, like my femur might do if subjected to severe impact, my mind chose to silently implode. It was January 21, 2002, the day my son turned eighteen. It was a day I will never forget.

I experienced what is currently called Major Depressive Disorder; it used to be called "severe" or "clinical" depression. Decades ago, they would have labeled it a "nervous break-down." Interestingly, I feel a stronger resonance for this later term, as it very closely describes my own experience: My mind was certainly broken, barely functioning at all. The thinking part was only a hair above a vegetative state; and my nervous system was definitely out of whack.

It took a full year of very gradual healing before I could return to work and start relearning how to complete simple office tasks—beginning with data entry, progressing to preparing standard letters where only the employee's name and address changed, to eventually using my writing skills to edit correspondence, and finally advancing to talking to colleagues on the phone to verify information contained in the letters—this "work-hardening" took place over a period of six months.

I was to revisit the state of depression several times over nine years, although those events were never as severe as the initial breakdown. Its gloomy specter hanging over me was enough to move me to get the necessary treatment at even the slightest sign of mental distress. That is the real trick—learning to recognize the earliest signals of potential overload or anxiety in time to thwart its progress and prevent full-on depression.

I became my own expert at this early-detection work—at identifying my personal canary in the coalmine, so to speak. I became a person who values mental health above everything else in life. Because if I don't have a healthy mind, the world holds no interest for me.

Depression is an insidious disease, lurking in the mind in places hidden from everyone, including yourself. But it can no longer hide from me. I have mastered its detection and I am back in charge.

I have learned that so long as I give my spirit what it wants and needs, as something that is essential to my whole person, I will continue to succeed at keeping a healthy balance in my life, far away from depression.

For years I struggled with this debilitating disease, a disease that is too scary for most people to talk about. I worked very hard at getting well and staying well. And I long to contribute my experience and hands-on knowledge if it can help another broken soul put a life back together. I long for my experience to be put to a larger use and purpose.

What if I could? What if someone who is struggling right now, who is desperately trying to hang on to some sense of normality, to a reality that she used to know, were to pick up this book? What if something about the words on these pages led one person to seek treatment, or led her to a resource that made a difference? Wouldn't that be worth doing? Oh, yes, it certainly would.

I am committed to contributing in some small way to positive change. I enjoy serving the higher good through the joy of expanding my abilities and talents. And I trust that my truth as explained in this book will be just the right thing for someone out there. Whoever you are, bless you!

It was the pacing. Back and forth, back and forth in front of my desk. I had just returned from my lunch break, alone, again. Even though I'd been working there for eleven years, I didn't have workplace friends—didn't know anyone well enough to go out to lunch with, to talk to about my work frustrations, the sense that I had bitten off more than I could chew when I accepted this new role. It had been four months and I still had not gotten to the bottom of all that it entailed; I felt that I was forever catching up, that I should be working on a different burning issue, one that I wasn't even aware of yet. I was given boxes of files that were now my responsibility and I still hadn't gotten through them all. I felt as though at any moment something in that box would explode in my face.

I was beginning to understand that this was a bigger job than I expected and I couldn't see my way through it. I felt trapped, with no one to call on for help. My manager was a high-level executive with much bigger fish to fry than my feelings of incompetence. I had convinced her during the interview that I was the best person for the job, so I wasn't about to let her know that she had made a mistake in hiring me.

In my world, a professional employee can handle things; she keeps trouble out of her boss's hands by anticipating and dealing with it first. I had been super competent in my previous jobs; this was my self-image and that of my colleagues and management.

> "Whether you believe something is possible or impossible, either way you'll be right."
>
> —Wayne Dyer

As I returned to my desk, I couldn't seem to focus as I tried to remember where I had left off. I sat at my computer in a daze, not knowing where to start or what to do. Was it the pile of letters that I should work on or e-mails? I couldn't make heads or tails of my desk, which was just a bunch of files and stacks of papers. My head was a blur. *Get a grip; just remember what you were doing before going for lunch,* I thought. But that was the problem. Every pile of work looked urgent. If I do this one, then I won't have time to get to that one. I felt a glassy-eyed paralysis come over me, a deer-in-the-headlights, brain-numbing sensation. I had been staring at my computer for the better part of an hour and I was no further ahead.

I couldn't sit there anymore. I had to get up and do something. I had to move. I began pacing, then hyperventilating. *Oh my, what is happening here?* I fretted. (I later learned that this was my brain engaging in the fight-or-flight response to protect me from the overwhelming stress. I was never much of a fighter, and there was no one that I could fight anyway. My mind chose to flee this untenable situation.)

I can't stay in this office—too suffocating, no windows, muted lighting, unreal. There are people outside my office doing work, as if everything is perfectly fine and normal! As if I'm not in a desperate panic! I must get out, go someplace else. But I need to tell someone that I'm leaving. But who? My boss was in another city. But my former manager, whom I'll call Arthur, worked just down the hall. *Maybe I'll ask him for help; he'll know what to do.*

I observed myself making my way to Arthur's office—*I can't believe I am doing this, going to him in my helpless state. How unprofessional.* But his friendly face and cheerful welcome were a blessing, a balm for my panic-stricken heart. *He can take charge now instead of me. That feels better already.* I shut the door as I entered the room (code for "this is serious"). When he asked how I was doing, I told him.

With my permission, he dialed the Employee Assistance Program's crisis line and the therapist at the end of the phone proceeded to talk me down. I started feeling calmer, no longer panicked, only fearful, lost, and tired—so tired. I would be okay after a few days of rest. Arthur suggested I take some time off, a week, or even three. "I don't need weeks; just a couple days will do," I said. I had been doing too much trying to learn my new job, including commuting two hours each way several times a week. I decided I would head home just as soon as I finished a few important letters.

Back in my office, I looked at the letters and drew a dead blank; I couldn't think how to start the letters, let alone finish them. I couldn't think at all. Instead, I deposited the letters with the secretary along with instructions and made my way home.

By the time I got to the house, twenty-five minutes away, I was utterly drained and exhausted. In the ensuing days, I tried to rest but couldn't sleep; my brain seemed on high alert, yet I couldn't get myself out of bed in the morning. I lost my appetite, and taking a shower was beyond my ability, the worst idea in the world. I didn't know what to do or say or how to act.

Having drawn a blank while sitting at my desk moments before leaving for home, my brain had stayed in Nowhere Land while my body had found its way home. I didn't understand what was happening to me, but at least I was safe now, feeling the protection of my home. I somehow got to my doctor's office—I have no recollection of that first visit—and thus began a yearlong battle with, and healing from, a nervous breakdown.

I had become traumatized by my workplace situation and my brain protected me by blocking all feelings from coming in or going out. That's one way to cope, but it turned me into a zombie, a body going through the motions of daily living but without a spirit inside. My soul had checked out, and I wished it had taken the rest of me with it.

My first experience of depression occurred in 2002 and lasted a year—which, as I now understand, is not unusually long. But try a year of this and see if you don't agree that it is the longest year of your life. It was, in fact, the darkest and loneliest time I have ever known, and it frightened me like nothing else could.

How Did This Happen to Me?
I was an average woman in her mid-forties with a good, responsible job in a large government organization. I lived with my husband, Robert, and two teenaged children, Caroline and Marcel. We had left the big city to live in a beautiful old home in the rolling hills of Cavan in central Ontario. It was a dream come true for us to live in the quiet country setting, surrounded

by nature and with little traffic. I was lucky to have the opportunity to follow my job in a corporate relocation to the small city of Peterborough.

By all accounts and appearances, I had a pretty good life. But at the risk of sounding cliché, I still felt that something was missing from my life; I did not feel fulfilled as a person and was forever searching for something more. But I made do and went through the paces, distracting myself with many hobbies and our idyllic surroundings. As it turned out, my situation was more serious than I knew.

After my breakdown, it was eleven months before I was able to successfully reenter the workplace. I say "successfully" because I experienced two failed attempts during that period. The first attempt, after about two months, made it clear that I was not ready for the workplace, when simply entering the building and touching the files on my desk caused severe anxiety. The second attempt was at the five-month mark, having requested a temporary project to gently test the waters rather than return to my previous job. I was forced to abandon that effort after a few days due to mounting anxiety caused by the realization that my cognitive abilities were quite restricted, such that I could not make sense of a straightforward task involving transcribing notes from a meeting.

This was only the beginning of the life changes that were to come for my family and me. (Depression affects the whole family, not just the person experiencing the illness.)

Finding My Way Back

It feels good to reveal to the world that I have come through depression and generalized anxiety and that I am doing well. I will always have the illness, but I've learned what it takes to manage it and how to lead a happy, balanced life. More than that, I have learned how to be an even better me because of the illness.

I have been to one of the darkest places of all and I know with certainty that I will do everything in my power not to return. For me, this depressive state wasn't about feeling sorry for myself or being sad; it was that my body's systems simply gave up. My mind quit because it could no longer tolerate the pressure of an overwhelming, isolating, and unsatisfying job.

> "We do not think ourselves into new ways of living; we live ourselves into new ways of thinking."
> —Richard Rohr

Something had to give. Life had erected a solid concrete wall for me to collide with head-on, because that was the only way to make me stop and reexamine my life and my choices.

I've come to know deeply that our spirits need feeding, and if we continue to starve them, they will eventually rebel, and they might be stronger than our will to ignore them. At least that seems to be what happened to me.

I didn't see it coming. Literally from one day to the next, I couldn't sleep, I couldn't get up in the morning, and I didn't care to look after myself, to take a shower, or to brush my teeth. I did not feel hunger, so I forced myself to eat at regular mealtimes. In truth, I didn't feel anything. I had no interest in my hobbies, felt no enjoyment when walking in the woods, which used to be a favorite activity, and had no desire to be with people, whom I sought to avoid at all costs. I couldn't even enjoy spending time with my children, whom I saw only every other weekend.

I experienced nothing—no joy, no laughter, no anything—only dull, flat darkness.

I was in a place that stole my identity and my personality, a place where I was nothing but an empty shell of a body going through the motions of day-to-day and minute-by-minute living. I was in a place where I believed I would remain forever stuck. I had no idea how to get out or if it was even possible to get out, and no one seemed able to help me.

I saw my family doctor at two-week intervals only to relay that there was no change in my "mood" and to learn that he also had nothing new for me. I had nothing to hang on to. "See you in two weeks" was my usual farewell, with a plastic smile on my face.

My eyes told of the vacancy inside, as if the person who had been renting space inside my body had suddenly up and left without telling the landlady. My soul was wide open, raw, naked, and completely exposed to a world that didn't care to know about it.

I worked hard at imitating a healthy person when doing errands or buying groceries and paying at the checkout. It was excruciating.

All I wanted was to disappear from existence. I felt safe only when inside our home, where I would stare out the window at nothing but the air floating by, thinking nothing, and feeling nothing.

After ten months of living in this near-vegetative state and with no help on the horizon, I began to accept that this would be my way of life from now on. I had given up on finding any help. I thought it best to accept the inevitable. It felt easier that way. None of the drugs I had been prescribed had any positive effect, and all had terrible side effects. I was without hope.

When I shared my thoughts with my then-twenty-one-year-old daughter, she answered, "Mom, that's not good enough." It's odd how her words snapped my awareness, like a switch being turned on.

This simple statement gave me a small measure of hope that somewhere, somehow, things could one day get better for me. (People need only a bit of hope to keep going.) I knew that I could not give up the fight just yet, for my family if not for myself. Though I did not believe my own thinking, corrupted as it was by the illness, I could rely on Caroline's sound thinking.

I decided to believe her instead of me, to trust that she spoke the truth. I hung on to her words as a beacon from the reality that I used to know. I credit my insightful daughter for having had a powerful effect on my eventually getting out of the muck.

I later learned that a medication I had been taking to prevent migraines might have triggered the depression. Four months after I stopped taking that drug, the depression began to lift.

It was an early December day while walking in the woods with Robert, as was our Sunday habit, when I first realized that I might be enjoying our outing a little bit. When getting back in the car, I thought, *Wait, I actually felt something on that walk!* This marked the start of my coming out of the depression.

It also was the beginning of a new existence of living *with* mental illness.

A New Approach

If I wanted a different outcome, a permanent different outcome, wouldn't I need a different approach to my healing? Because clearly, the standard, Western approach to healing I had been following was not working for me. I had suffered my third depression "event" in less than eight years, and I wanted a lasting solution that really worked. That's when I invited Divine Spirit to take the lead.

My silent request went something like this: "Heavenly Spirit, you have the power to make all things happen. Show me how to heal, show me how to get better for good. I'm so tired of repeating the same story. You must take the lead because I haven't got a clue where to start. I will follow you. But you have to be in charge. I will follow wherever you take me." This was my prayer.

Now, don't get the idea that I relinquished all interest in the case—not for a minute! In fact, I was mightily committed to every little step the future held for me. And I was also committed to letting Spirit guide those steps. I relinquished control of *how* I would move forward and I put my trust in the Divine, knowing that the Holy Spirit was in a better position than I to know what I needed to get well and to stay well.

My resolve became the driving force. Growing up, I was known in my family for being a very determined girl (not to say a stubborn child!). Well, wouldn't you know that this very trait would be key not only to helping me survive a depressed mental state but also to thriving because of it. But I am getting ahead of myself.

Let's return to the fall of 2009 when I found myself strapped with generalized anxiety and PTSD.

My self-image was frail and my inner core felt damaged. This was the state I found myself in when looking into that hallway mirror as I handed over the reins to Spirit. My fragility was due in great part to my years-long struggle with depression; but it was also grounded in the trials and tribulations of my life, especially starting from a difficult childhood and problem teen years.

Who among us doesn't know someone who has a difficult background and yet appears to be getting along in his or her life quite well? It can certainly happen that way. But this wasn't how my story unfolded; my background led me to and through depression. I don't know about those other people, and I wish them well with all my heart. I only know for certain how my background shaped the person that I am today. As human beings, we are given challenges to live through, and I know that my childhood struggles were mild in comparison to many. In the end, I am grateful for the way it all turned out.

> "Energy cannot be created or destroyed, but energy can be transformed."
> —Master Chunyi Lin

Thanks to undergoing periods of psychotherapy over the years, I understood that my inner foundation was indeed shaky.

According to my cognitive behavior therapist, I needed to rebuild my self-esteem. But how the heck was I expected to do that? I wasn't offered an instruction book with a step-by-step program for achieving this, though I desperately wanted one.

I began to see this as a new challenge and took on the job of learning how to strengthen my self-esteem; I figured that a healthier self-image would naturally follow. It made sense that this would be a necessary starting point for my overall healing.

I had always admired my sister Anne, four years my elder, as a strong and super-confident person. She seemed sure of herself and single-minded when going after what she wanted in life. Nothing got in her way. Of four sisters, she is closest to me in age and we shared many interests. But compared to her, I felt there was no way I could ever be so strong, even if I knew how to go about it (which I did not!).

My therapist suggested that I start by doing the things I enjoyed most, noting how the experience felt, and in particular, noticing any mood changes after the activity. The theory was that if I enjoyed doing a certain thing, then I was probably good at it (because we seldom enjoy doing what we are not at least somewhat good at). And this could be a positive move toward elevating my self-esteem. I followed her advice. Because, truthfully, what else did I have to go on?

I focused on activities that produced something tangible, like doing a craft or a sewing project. I recorded the result, posting pictures on my private blog, which I used for journaling my progress. I recorded even the smallest of successes as I went through my day. (*Success* is used here in the broadest sense to mean any forward movement toward building a healthier picture of myself.) The more I created tangible things, the more successes I could record. And my list of "achievements" began to grow.

The reason it was important to make note of even the tiniest success is that I was actually training my brain and my subconscious to form a new image of Michèle and her value, her worthiness. I needed to feed my brain new information, using as many methods as possible, in an effort to outweigh the thick layers of old and untrue beliefs that had built up over the years. I was replacing the sludge with higher, lighter, and truer information.

Well, if that's what it took, then I would have fun with it! My blogging space became a creative place to explore. I learned how to post pictures of my creations and other upbeat images (like my daughter running carefree through a field of gorgeous chartreuse-yellow canola plants with a big clear-blue sky above) and I played around with colors. Without conscious effort, I was learning something of the new blogging technology as I went along. It was pure play, but my natural curiosity in learning to use the software would prove important when I returned to work.

The next step was to enlarge the type of activities that I engaged in, which would serve to expand my repertoire of successes. Little by little, and item by item, the scope of my achievements began to emerge and multiply. Soon, I started believing that I was good not only at sewing garments and knitting projects, activities that I had been practicing for many years, but also at planning and cooking great meals, at designing and fabricating original window treatments, at overseeing renovations and decorating our new home, at selecting tasteful furniture and fixtures, and at coordinating colors. I started believing that I was good at many things.

Each day, I would record those small and not-so-small successes. Because, should I one day be inclined to revert to my old, negative thought patterns—which I fully expected to do at some point, as that was still my brain's default position—I would need proof to the contrary. My journal entries about my new reality would help me get back on track. Also, seeing these things written down not only made them more real to my brain, it also made it possible for me to believe something good about myself. Hey, wasn't it written down? Then it must be true, right? At least, that's how my brain would perceive it. And I wanted so much to believe.

Through art and beauty, through practicing creativity in my chosen art forms, by doing with purpose what I enjoyed, I eventually pulled myself out of a negative self-image.

Today, I enjoy a healthy self-image. While I strive for humility of spirit, I no longer downplay or degrade my abilities—not to myself nor to the world at large. The process wasn't easy and it wasn't instant, but if you've suffered with depression, you know that any relief is like a miracle.

In these pages, I'm going to share my miracle with you and hope that you can find a way to make such a miracle happen in your own life. Depression is a big obstacle, no doubt, but remember that it is just that: an obstacle. It is not you. And it is not your life.

When I made the decision to ask the Divine to take hold of my hand and lead me on a new path, I did not hold a special ceremony nor make a formal request. No, it all happened in a flash when I looked at myself in the hall mirror and thought, *This is going to be the last time I suffer this way!*

It was as if my soul jumped in through the mirror to stand with the Holy Spirit looking back at me and together, they agreed: "Okay, let's do this!"

Why not start with practicing the same techniques I was learning for transforming wishes into reality? Why not work at attracting positive universal flow into my current problem?

I was learning that what you think about expands, as well as other law-of-attraction principles (see the Resources section, on page 197). "Yes," I said to myself and to Spirit, "let's you and I put those notions into practice starting right now."

I would begin by focusing my mind and attention on expanding and trusting my intuition. I would hone my intuition like a fine-tuned instrument; I had confidence in that, at least. Not that I would be announcing this seemingly radical approach far and wide because frankly, I didn't care for the skepticism I was sure to encounter. I also didn't feel the need to justify my decision.

It was an agreement between the Holy Spirit and me, and that was enough for me. And I certainly didn't share any of this with Robert, who, despite his many wonderful qualities, might have led the skeptics' charge.

I decided to trust the insight, although the word *decide* is not quite right, because there was no thinking involved here, more like a felt sense, an inner knowing that transcended thinking to land directly in the core of my being. I just knew and trusted it.

"It is a powerful statement to God that we want the graces of contemplation, that delightful experience of God's presence and love. It opens the door wide to let God act freely in us, especially through the Spirit's gifts of wisdom and understanding."

—M. Basil Pennington

I put my trust in Spirit and I resolved to follow wherever it led. Yes, I was taking what would surely be seen as a questionable or an experimental path for a serious medical condition. But since there was no better alternative on offer, I went for it.

My task now was to sharpen my instincts and to really tune into all of my senses, to practice hearing with my body versus my head, to listen with intent to my inner voice. I was grateful to have prior knowledge of how to listen to what my body had to say and how to pay attention to what my instincts perceived, thanks to a workshop I'd attended decades ago on "Focusing."

I needed to sharpen these tools so I could better capture Divine guidance in whatever form it might take; I didn't want to miss a thing. Every clue would be important.

I mentioned that I was experimenting with applying law-of-attraction principles. I was playing with the idea to help me get some house-related projects and decorating done, having recently moved from a century home in the country to a modern bungalow in the city. I was at a loss on several of those projects. I was no stranger to painting walls, but I had no idea how to select paint colors for an open-concept house where the walls all connected visually. It was quite a learning curve for me, and I wanted some help.

From some of Sonia Choquette's teachings, I was learning how to pay close attention to my inner voice and how to invite Spirit to take an active role in my day-to-day life. I had been practicing by putting clear requests "out there" and observing the answers. There was nothing too serious in this activity so far. Mostly, I was observing synchronicity in action almost daily: bumping into the right people at the exact right time, being guided in finding things I had misplaced and thought lost, getting needed information from total strangers, and enjoying delightful connection with like-minded ones.

I was already working on expanding and trusting my intuition. But now I was turning my mental health—thus my entire life—over to the Divine's charge.

Instinct told me I needed to practice connecting my spirit with the Divine in order to achieve my goal.

• I practiced daily morning meditation to connect with Spirit while staying firmly grounded. I would invite the Divine into my body—not my head—with the intention of obtaining perfect balance of heart, body, and soul each and every day. This is still how I start my days, often envisioning how I want the day to be.

• I did a daily visualization exercise to picture myself thinking positive thoughts and getting positive outcomes. This was part of training my mind to think differently, and I was rigorous in sustaining this new mental discipline.

• I wrote daily in my journal and frequently went walking in nature, often combining the two activities. My favorite spot to journal was a bench at the edge of a creek in a nearby forested park. I had read that being near flowing water is healthy for the soul and the body (something about negative ions increasing the level of serotonin in the brain and boosting your mood and energy).

• I scheduled time at least every other day to engage in vigorous physical exercise and other pleasant activities to stimulate positive brain chemistry.

• I created a private blog to document my every success and capture my progress in a creative and playful way.

• I played at imagination games and tried to capture my emotions with coloring.

• And most of all, I practiced positive thinking using Cognitive Behavior Therapy (CBT) techniques at every moment of every day.

The routine kept me busy, but still I wanted more. I signed up for a nine-week online course for solidifying my partnership with the Divine and to do good works. I wanted to do my little bit to help balance the world's heavy burden from the not-so-good side. (See the Resources section on page 197.) At a cost of $400 on my seriously restricted budget, this was a huge leap of faith, one that my head was having a hard time accepting but that my instincts registered as a definite next step for me. So I jumped in. I waited in great anticipation for the first class to start the following week.

A few weeks after the course began, during a morning meditation, I realized that my leap of faith had been exactly that—a huge leap through making a tangible demonstration of my faith (what is more tangible than money when you're not making much?) and my commitment to the Divine, and to allowing it to take hold of my life. In Oprah Winfrey's book *What I Know for Sure*, she mentions one of her favorite quotes, by W.H. Murray: "The moment one definitely commits oneself, then Providence moves, too." How apt.

This was a concrete, deal-making exercise to illustrate that my healing process was to be an equal partnership; it demonstrated to the universe that I was willing to put in as much as I would take out. I'm convinced that my signing up for this course was a watershed moment in my path to new health.

Recovery became my full-time job.

I read books that taught me I was not an aberration. I learned I am not anti-social but simply an introvert, and how that explains why I enjoy spending time alone, just me and my own company. I used to think that something was wrong with me and that I should be more inclined to socialize.

In *Party of One: The Loners' Manifesto*, author Anneli Rufus validates my feelings regarding social interactions and how I relate to the world. This book was God-sent, no question about it. I learned that being an introvert is not so weird. In fact, looking back through history, we learn that many great inventors, explorers, and creators were introverts. It's just different from what most people see in a world designed by and for extroverts—while we introverts are busy being ourselves and not paying a whole lot of attention to what others are about. I learned that for me to be well, I *need* solitude, and that this is a legitimate desire.

Another book that ranks high in the selected-by-Spirit-especially-for-me category is Matthew Kelly's *Perfectly Yourself: 9 Lessons for Enduring Happiness.* Oh, how this book saved my bacon. (I'll explain in detail in chapter nine, Daily Structure, how this author guided my every step.)

A third book that helped me in my healing journey is Tom Harpur's *Finding the Still Point.* It helped me to marry favorite secular practices with insights gleaned from the teachings of the Gospels. I deepened my understanding of God's grace in my life, how we are "often brought to a grinding halt" in order to discover our true nature, how if we are lucky indeed, we can experience our higher self as being one with the Savior (the greater power, the universe).

> "O God give me light in my heart and light in my tongue, and light in my hearing and light in my sight, and light in my feeling and light in all my body, and light before me and light behind me. Give me, I pray Thee, light on my right hand and light on my left hand and light above me and light beneath me; O Lord, increase light within me and give me light, and illumine me."
>
> — A prayer ascribed to Muhammad, quoted by Tom Harpur

I also learned that creativity is a crucial component for my being well, that my soul needs creative expression as much as my body needs food and sleep. I set up a permanent space in our house where I could play to my heart's desire, and I made time for creativity in my daily life (see chapter three, The Role of Creativity).

Nurturing My Spirit to Heal My Soul

Each morning, I would ask my spirit what it needed that day. Did it want to create something in my sewing workroom? Cocoon on the couch with a novel and a cup of tea? Take a brisk walk with the dogs? Sit on a park bench by the river and write in my journal? Or was it drawn more to settling in a coffee shop and being among people as I wrote on my blog?

I would choose an option based solely on my gut response and follow through. Later that day, I would write about my chosen activity and record how it had affected my mood, whether I felt better, the same, or worse as a result.

I continued to follow my heart's desire as my top priority, and this began to nurture my spirit. I chose soothing activities every day and focused my complete attention on them to distract me from the repetitive, old thoughts about my worthlessness and the futility of trying to get better. This was my third bout with mental illness, and I knew from my reading that the pattern for my life was quite probably already set. When push came to shove, I held little hope of changing that.

I determined not to listen to those thoughts, choosing instead to engage in uplifting activities. I did this in spite of my low mood, in which I did not feel like doing anything at all, let alone something good. But I pushed on and disciplined myself to engage in an activity every day, and I recorded what changes I could notice in my mental state, even when there was no change.

A SPIRIT-CENTERED LIFE

Two years prior to my nervous breakdown, on the trip home following a weeklong spiritual retreat in 2000, I was graced with a crystal-clear view of how my life had been carefully orchestrated by the Holy Spirit from the start. Here I was at age forty-three continuing on my sacred path, which began at my birth (if not before). This was quite a revelation considering the many years I spent disconnected from God, through the expected teenage heartbreak, a broken marriage, postpartum and general depression, and loneliness. It's truly a thing of beauty how, in an instant, I saw my spiritual path with such lucidity—yet another gift of grace.

It all started when I was a newborn baby at my christening. In those days, the mother stayed home and did not attend the baptismal ceremony; the godmother carried the infant to church and held her to receive the sacrament. In the eyes of the Church, my godmother was my protector and the one ultimately responsible for my spiritual life.

Tante Liliane did not disappoint. She was the kindest, most generous woman, forever helping those in need. A few years before her passing, she told me how at my christening, she had made a silent prayer request of the Holy Spirit on my behalf; she asked that the Spirit watch over me and protect me from harm. You see, my godmother knew that I was to live in a troubled household with an abusive, alcoholic father, and that I might need the extra protection.

On my way home from the retreat, from my seat on that inter-city bus, I suddenly understood that her request indeed had been answered. And I know that Divine Spirit continues to watch over me. (Thank you, *merci, Tante Liliane.*)

A few months after my christening and with five children in tow, my mother took her chances while my father was at work and left him and everything behind. She feared for her own life, but especially for her children's well-being. Some people see her bravery, but she saw her escape as simply doing what was necessary.

We travelled by train from Montréal to her parents' home in Fauquier, a hamlet in Northern Ontario six hundred miles away, where we stayed for a time while Mom sorted out her next step in settling her own family.

As a support to my mother, one of her sisters and husband took me in and treated me as the daughter they never had (they had two older sons). They became very attached to me and would have gladly kept me for good if my mother had allowed it. I stayed with them for four months, from the age of six months to ten months, and in later years, it was common for me to spend extended periods of time with them, especially during summers.

The reason I'm telling this story is that my aunt and uncle were devout Roman Catholics (by all appearances to my young self, anyway). Although my own family was also Catholic, we were less inclined to bring religion or faith into the household. We went to church on Sundays, attended Catholic schools, ate fish on Fridays, and that's where religion ended for us. We were Catholic by culture, like all French-Canadians at the time, more than by faith.

By contrast, my aunt and uncle's house was God-filled. We said grace at mealtimes, there were Catholic icons in every room, we prayed the rosary in the evenings at seven o'clock along with a radio broadcast, and we sang religious songs as we went about our day.

My aunt made plaster statues and crucifixes from rubber molds and painted them, selling these door to door to her neighbors and in nearby towns and villages. I remember a particular statue of Jesus that stood twelve inches tall with a freshly painted, cherry-red heart, drying in the center of the kitchen table, placed far from curious little fingers. But when no one was around, my four-year-old legs easily climbed onto a kitchen chair to touch the irresistibly shiny heart. Later, my aunt smiled at the red smear on my white blouse as I tried to deny my transgression. She was sweet and kind to me, never punishing me, not even raising her voice.

Growing up, I delighted in spending long periods with my aunt and uncle. They were eager to drive the two hours to come fetch me and welcome me back to my second home. Returning to my family after these visits was always a rude awakening. Glad to be reunited with my mother, it was hard for my little girl's spirit to adjust to a household filled with rambunctious older siblings who resented the special attention I was receiving, while they did chores and earned extra money for the family by babysitting. But for me, these summers away were the highlight of my childhood.

In fact, the time spent with my aunt and uncle laid the foundation in my child's heart for the warmth and peace of living in the company of Christ.

My family left the Church when I was eleven years old, and I spent my teen and adult years searching for that missing something; there had to be something more to life! When, at the age of forty-three, I finally caught up with that something, I found that it was God. I had trouble saying the word out loud at first, because it made me feel nerdy and pathetic due to my conditioned thinking from years spent criticizing Christianity and churchgoers. Back then, I saw religion as a crutch for those who were too weak to stand on their own. How judgmental! I now knew that my search was over and that I had found what I had been yearning for. I had come home. What a classic tale, even though it felt mightily original as I experienced it.

I felt such inner peace, a deep knowing that I was where I belonged. Like a calm, spirit-filled lake, I had found the source where I began and to which I would one day return. It was like finding a long-lost treasure for which I had spent a lifetime hunting, without a map, and where I found the richest of gold mines by happenstance. You might suspect that my finding God right where I stood was not by chance but by design. And I feel blessed at having been invited to join his universal family.

Severe depression came for an extended visit two years later, and I forgot all about Spirit, my newfound treasure. I spent most of the next decade going in and out of darkness, surviving as I could without medication because the variety of drugs that were prescribed for me didn't help.

A BLENDED FAITH

While I have a strong Christian faith, I also embrace the notion of co-creation as presented by law-of-attraction principles (the idea that what you focus on expands, and the power of positive beliefs). It makes so much sense, particularly when outcomes are witnessed, and it supports a joyful existence while on earth. That's good enough for me!

I have witnessed too many manifestations of co-creation in my own life—some of which I have tried to explain in this book—to be anything but convinced.

I also have experienced personally the awesome healing power of the Holy Spirit. I recall the morning after She had come to me while I slept. It was the second day of a weeklong retreat at a Catholic center in Sutton, Québec, 2010. I was blown away. Gobsmacked! I had gone to bed resolute on leaving the retreat the very next morning because of my disagreement with things the priest and retreat leader had said about faithless Quebecers. I was angry with him for speaking his personal biases the way he had, and I felt that he was out of bounds, in essence telling us how we should think. I reacted strongly to his words but said nothing, as this was a silent retreat and his words were not up for discussion, in any case. This was not my first retreat here, but I was not impressed this time.

The next morning, I was surprised to awaken feeling refreshed and with a new heart. The raging anger from the previous evening was gone, vanished! I simply understood things with a new clarity. I instantly forgave the priest for his opinions, for wasn't he just a man? Shouldn't he be allowed his imperfections too? Now, I am not one to easily give up on my ideas or beliefs. Only I no longer found anger or negativity in my heart. None. Nothing but a sense of peace resided there now. If you have ever experienced the Lord's peace in your soul, you know there is nothing else like it. It is a recognizable, pure state of utter calm and peacefulness. This was an awesome gift indeed, to be directly ministered to by the Holy Spirit. It left me feeling very special, and humble, that my little life and human concerns could warrant the attention of the Holy Spirit. This "happening" not only reversed my decision to abandon the retreat, but it served to open my mind to the very real existence of God (by whatever name you choose to call this otherworldly, Spirit-based, omnipresent superpower). *Oh my!* I thought, *He really is true! It's all true!*

And by the way, for any skeptics reading this, my mind was absolutely not involved in my change of heart. The change happened without my mind's awareness. It was only through observing my feelings upon waking—with much surprise, I might add—that my mind understood what had taken place overnight; the change already had happened.

Holy Spirit must have known that opening my heart and mind was a necessary first step to receiving the teachings that awaited me that week; this particular retreat focused on the foundational beliefs of the Catholic faith. My own connection to Catholicism had ended in my youth, so I had some catching up to do. We never discussed matters of faith in my family, nor was there any such talk in the Church back then. I remembered some of the rules and traditions, such as confession and fasting one hour before Mass (same as for going swimming) and eating fish on Fridays. But I didn't understand the "what for" of those rules.

The retreat filled my information gap and more. It healed my soul and made it possible for me to recommit to being a happy, practicing Christian. But, years later, I found that something was still missing. It appeared that so long as I was attending a retreat, which I still enjoy every year or two, and as long as I was surrounded by people with a deep and active spirituality and faith, I felt fulfilled, well-nourished, and content. But once back in my everyday world, where I am a member of a large Catholic parish, I eventually begin to feel a void in my relationship with God, and a longing to share my joy in faith.

I want to step boldly into my faith, and writing this book is part of that effort. I don't want to be shy about my faith anymore; I want to be fearless in my beliefs.

Recently, I recalled how close to Spirit I had felt in 2010 when I diligently practiced law-of-attraction (LOA) principles. I relied implicitly on Divine Spirit for showing me the way out from depression. My inner ears were attuned to Spirit's ways, and I enjoyed regular confirmation through her active participation in my life. I craved that kind of intimacy. Today, I've learned to integrate LOA practices with my Catholic ones. Personally, I don't view this as conflicting; to the contrary, I feel the two practices complete each other.

I enjoy the duality of so-called new-age thinking combined with traditional religiosity. For me, it fills the void left open by a traditional Catholic faith. By charting my own spiritual path, I am left feeling joyfully fulfilled. And for me, that's the whole point of faith. It also propels me to help others along their lives' unique paths.

"Finally, beloved, whatever is true, whatever is honorable, whatever is just, whatever is pure, whatever is pleasing, whatever is commendable, if there is any excellence and if there is anything worthy of praise, think about these things. Keep on doing the things that you have learned and seen in me, and the God of peace will be with you."
—Philippians 4:8–9

SPIRIT GUIDANCE

Ever wonder what it feels like to be guided by Divine Spirit? I will always remember one such experience from a few years ago. It was subtle but unmistakable. Describing how I knew it for sure is perhaps more difficult.

It felt like effortless activity, smooth and seamless. It was speaking the exact right words at the right moment, words that came into my brain (through inner hearing) just as I was opening my mouth, words of pure compassion and caring, grace and harmony, that were *from* me but not *of* me. And a feeling that I was observing myself—in this case in the role of family facilitator—delivering the magic of true mastery when I was but a novice.

It was knowing for sure that I was inside a perfectly aligned moment, which in this case lasted several hours. For me, the sweetness of the experience changed the quality of the rest of the week because I knew that Spirit was with me, with us.

This is how the story took place.

We were five sisters who had come together to spend a week relaxing at a rental cottage, and to connect with the love we shared for our mom who had passed away recently. On the second evening, we gathered in the living area to talk about our expectations for the week and to share what we each hoped to take away from our time together. With my sisters' permission, I began the exchange with a prayer and the expressed desire that Mom's spirit might be among us.

While the evening progressed in a congenial manner, I noticed that one of my sisters, I'll call her sister B, appeared less enthusiastic with the process. In fact, when it came to her turn, she opted not to share her thoughts.

As the evening wrapped up, some called it a night while others stayed to chat quietly.

The following day at supper, sister A suggested that we might engage in a second sharing exercise, asking a different question this time. Because I had initiated the previous evening's activity, the question was directed at me. I responded favorably but only if everyone was in agreement.

That's when the verbal explosion went off. Sister B passionately defended her right not to be pressured into doing something that made her feel uncomfortable. With that, she left the room, upset, and went outside. Several minutes went by as the rest of us sat in stunned silence.

To me, this situation was not completely unexpected, because I had noticed sister B's less-than-enthusiastic participation the night before. While wanting to give her the room to be upset on her own, I also felt compelled to go to her should she want support. And I didn't want her imagining the rest of us talking about her.

She stood in the yard by the fire pit, out of sight from the cottage's picture window. I explained that sister A had not intended to impose her ideas, nor had she meant to hurt sister B or make her uncomfortable. While I agreed the suggestion possibly lacked sensitivity, it had been made innocently enough.

It was clear to me that no harm had been intended, based on sister A having immediately expressed regret over the incident to the rest of us. I explained this to sister B and asked if she would be willing to discuss the matter privately with sister A. She agreed but didn't want to go inside.

And thus began my role as facilitator and go-between, lasting well into the evening. Especially when sister C decided she wanted a turn in talking with sister B.

I had no background or prior experience as a facilitator or negotiator. None. Yet I was able to play the role well and without great effort—but only because Holy Spirit guided my every move. I felt a deep sense of calm for the length of this potentially volatile situation, concerning three women who mean a great deal to me.

I did not feel especially tired after what should have completely drained this introvert of emotional energy. I only hoped that my sisters would succeed in mending their hurts well enough to enjoy the rest of the week together.

I thanked Spirit for her guidance during and after the "proceeding" because it was that clear to me that I was not doing this on my own. Others noticed and praised me for my seemingly natural role.

It's important to note that the facilitator role is not my default position generally, and especially not in my family as the second youngest sibling.

I know, without a doubt, that I was not alone as facilitator that evening. I felt like a trained professional; I knew exactly what to do and say, and when to say nothing and just listen. I experienced a deep level of empathy, understanding, and patience that I wish came naturally to me. I'm working on those qualities, but that evening, I didn't have to try—it was all there within me.

I hope this explanation helps the reader to better understand how I could tell that I was being guided. Others may well have a different experience of Divine guidance.

How Can God Do What He Does?

The question is often posed: How could God possibly keep track of all the people on this earth and their individual situations and prayers? For me, that's not so difficult to imagine. I remember as a child learning the words *omnipresent* and *omniscient*—both of which have stood the test of time in terms of explaining how God does it. I learned that, because God is not an entity like we are but is instead made up of energy and pure spirit, that's how he can be everywhere and anywhere at the same time, like smoke, or like an idea gone viral that shoots out in every direction simultaneously. I also learned that our human mind is incapable of fully understanding what or who God is, that we should just accept him for what he says he is. I'm willing to do that, but I was born with a pretty trusting nature, too trusting at times as my husband might attest. (I feel fortunate for that these days.)

People like to raise objections regarding God's effectiveness in coming to our aid, citing all the prayers they send his way, seemingly without response. But do they surrender all control? Do they let go of expectations? Do they honor their spiritual Father by letting him be the one in charge; do they agree that he has command of their lives? In my experience, this is the hardest concept for people to wrap their minds around—in reality, it's not their minds they need to call on, it's their hearts and souls. This is the hardest barrier for most people to get through, to let go of it all while not being tied to outcomes. God's ideas of an outcome and method are likely quite different from ours.

It's important to check how deep our faith goes, because someone with total faith in God and in *his ways,* someone who trusts God to do only what's best for them, because he loves them like his own child, probably already is enjoying the fruits of his or her faith, along with a joyful dose of God's grace and blessings.

That's just the way of God. Nothing compares to the ultimate joy that is experienced when you know to the bottom of your toes (and soul) that God is present in your life, and acting in it along with you every day. Sweetness and purity.

It altogether feels like a symbiotic partnership because we each have a part to play: God can't do what he wants to accomplish without you, and you can't do much without him. Sure, God *could* do whatever he wants, but he chooses to work through us. It's the deal he cut, that he would only help us when we asked, and he fixed it so that we would need his help to accomplish great things, to accomplish all he designed us to be and do, so that we would need him.

It sounds so simple once a person chooses acceptance. In truth, it *is* that simple, so simple it is pure beauty. And the joy, the joy brings tears to the eyes. How can something this simple work so completely, so effortlessly, and so perfectly? Well, I also learned early on that God is perfection. Maybe that's why it feels that way.

One more thing: I learned how to train ego to take its rightful place, as my servant and not my boss. Ever wonder what can take place in your life with a passionate desire for serving others, combined with God's grace? See for yourself how seamlessly things begin falling into place. Worth a test run?

HOLY SPIRIT AS PERSONAL LIFE COACH

That's what I feel I received from Holy Spirit in 2010: a personal, extended life coach for straightening my life, enjoying a new, healthy path, on which I enjoyed becoming fully healed and placing my renewed focus on creating a sustainable, fulfilling life. To me, that is nothing short of miraculous considering where I had been and was coming from.

The right medication was instrumental in changing my brain chemistry to enable me to have a fighting chance at sustaining my healthy thinking for the long term; without it, even though I knew the mechanics of thinking healthy thoughts, it would have been an arduous and constant battle in my own head guaranteed to wear me down over time. I believe I could not have achieved the level of success I enjoy without the right drugs.

By the same token, without the rest of my get-well package, the will to establish a strong discipline for retraining my brain to ignite positive thinking, to purposefully incorporate creativity into my daily life, to sharpen and trust my intuition, to shape my desired reality—all of which I kick-started and established before taking the medication—I also could not have achieved such a complete overhaul and reached overarching success.

The magic resulted from the alchemy of three sources:

1. Healing and leadership from Divine Spirit
2. The right medication (chemical mix) for my brain
3. A trusting, determined, and disciplined personality equipped with responsive tools.

I am convinced that I would not be enjoying the fulfilling life I have today were it not for those three pieces coming together at the right time, like a perfect storm.

I thank God every day for my mental health and well-being; I never want to take that gift for granted, because I know deeply how precious it is and what a bonus it is to have my very own Divine Spirit lighting my path. Every day, I ask God to show me ways in which I can give back by helping others, that he help me do good according to his will, not mine. I consciously and gladly relinquish control over my life in exchange for his guidance.

I have found that for the everyday person, the notion of relinquishing control is the most difficult part about faith, the act of giving up control over every aspect of their lives; they fear the unknown and what God might have them do (or not do), perhaps having to give up things or people they dearly love.

I remember that feeling well from only a few years ago. I was willing to give him control over the entirety of my life except for one thing: I was not willing to leave my marriage, end of story. And that is precisely what I told God. He could have anything except for the authority over my marriage. But once I understood that God had no intention of taking me away from my marriage, that in fact, he wanted me to stay and to love Robert right, I was no longer afraid of handing over the reins. And that's when life really took off for me in the utmost direction.

I came to understand that God loves me more than anything, and if that is so, then why would he do anything that was anything but good for me? Wouldn't he only do things that served me well? Naturally, he would. There was nothing to fear in that; on the contrary, I wanted those very things for myself, too. That's when the penny dropped for me. Then it became easy to follow him and do his will—that is, when I was graced with such clarity of knowledge.

What a sweet pleasure life has become; quite a contrast to the life I used to know.

MY BIGGEST GOD WINK

As I grew spiritually, and as my faith blossomed through a steady stream of nourishment from both traditional and leading-edge thinkers, I began to question my life and especially my marriage.

Let me tell you something about my husband. He is solid. Robert has the strongest personal moral code I have ever encountered. He's also a polite and gallant man. And he chooses not to align himself with a particular faith or belief system. Being fairly new to my own faith conversion, and thrilled as I was to have found fulfillment in my lifelong quest, my judgmental mind had unfairly concluded that my way was the true path and that unless Robert signed up to a similar journey, I couldn't stay and still be true to myself. (How wrong I was, and what a treasure I nearly gave away.)

I had so many questions. Was I meant to be in this marriage considering my insatiable hunger for spiritual growth? Wouldn't my faith expand better if my life partner shared a similar Christian faith? What was I doing in this relationship at this time in my faith journey? Did I still belong here? Was I staying in this fifteen-year marriage out of fear? Out of guilt? Out of a sense of responsibility? Out of love? Was I meant to continue in this marriage?

My heart and mind wrestled with these questions, and my soul was in constant battle, trying to grasp what was best for me, for Robert, for us.

I struggled and struggled until I couldn't think straight. I was confused and I grew tired of the dance. I wanted to understand what was expected of me, what God expected of me. I wanted to do the right thing and I also believed that my ultimate purpose in life was to grow spiritually—and I felt that these two premises were at odds. I felt desperate. I finally asked God point blank, what do you want from me? What am I supposed to do here?

It was a Saturday afternoon in early June 2010, a few weeks after attending the "You Can Do It" conference in Toronto. I was in my office/meditation room listening to an online interview

with one of the authors I had heard speak at the conference—
I don't recall the author or the topic. Part way through the
recording, as I pointed my mouse to increase the volume, the
recording somehow got switched to another channel—literally
and figuratively. What happened next absolutely floored me.

I was now tuned to a radio call-in show hosted by Sonia
Choquette. The caller was expounding on her question, and the
more she spoke, the more I realized that her query matched
mine exactly, word for word! It blew me away.

The caller was a mom in her mid-thirties, a strong believer
in her spirituality who actively practiced listening to her sixth
sense, her inner knowing. Her husband was a good man and he
was a nonbeliever. And while he did not object to her teaching
her faith to their children, he, himself, wanted no part of it. She
had tried everything to get him interested in her faith, to no
avail. She was going through a heart-wrenching inner battle and
was on the verge of breaking up her marriage because she felt so
strongly that her faith had to come first.

The answer from Sonia's lips was like angel music to my ears
(and I hope to the caller's as well). This is what Sonia told her:
"Your husband may not believe the same things you do, but
your job is not to judge him; your job is not to change him; your
job is simply to love him. Love him as he is."

Hearing these words felt like the heavens had opened up into
my whole being. I was instantly filled with pure joy and a sense
of peace (God's signature). My heart was elated and my mind
understood that the universe had just answered me! I knew
from deep in my soul and with every cell in my body that this
was the reply to my question.

I felt free and satisfied and calm and complete and joyful, beyond words.

I would simply love Robert, that's what I would do. Love him for who he was, exactly *as* he was. End of conundrum. End of my inner battle.

However, I now had a different problem. For all of my adult life I had struggled with opening up my heart fully. It would hurt whenever someone got too close to my vulnerable core, so I learned to keep that part of my heart protected. I knew this was in response to the repeated rejection I had experienced as a child, but that knowledge did not help to heal the old wound.

But now, I understood something about my marriage that I hadn't known before—I was in this union to learn how to love completely, with my whole self. And as a supplemental benefit, it would allow my wound to heal.

If God wanted me here to learn this thing, then I was ready to trust that I would be safe in opening my heart fully to Robert. The more I opened my heart and gave kindness to my husband, the more love was returned.

My marriage is indeed teaching me to love better. And it is teaching me to trust. In truth, Robert and I are teaching each other. I couldn't hope for a more perfect match!

This experience was one of purity and perfection.

LISTENING TO MY INNER VOICE

I've always felt a certain connection to my instincts, that internal sense of knowing regarding people, places, or things. I attended a weekend workshop in 1987 by Eugene T. Gendlin on Focusing, which helped me to better understand and further develop this type of knowing. I learned how to pinpoint what my body was telling me through using my internal senses. The workshop taught me how to recognize the difference between being spot-on in my sensing and not quite hitting the mark. It taught me how to focus with intent and to listen from within my body. I learned how to connect with the inner sense of an issue, a circumstance, or an emotion. I learned to distinguish between when it was right to move forward and when it was better to walk away.

Gendlin calls this process "getting a felt sense"; gaining a better understanding of my body's response helps me make better decisions and choices, while growing in self-knowledge.

I found the technique especially useful for letting go of negativity that the body holds onto and for neutralizing bad memories, emotions, and thoughts. It can be used successfully in healing old wounds that our "pain body" retains, as Eckhart Tolle calls our body of experience.

Most of all, I learned to identify and trust my sensing abilities and my inner voice. I've heard it referred to as the little voice inside of us, but mine is big and sonorous; it has no problem making itself heard, and it continues to serve me well.

On Knowing My Purpose

One day I was sitting in my living room with my best friend, Sue, and a friend of hers whom I was only beginning to know, chatting about the challenge of leading a spiritual life when mixed in with the business of life, and how the law of attraction can support our personal practice. I mentioned that when we have a sense of our own life's purpose, it becomes easier to be selective about choices that come our way, thereby reducing the load. I felt that, while many opportunities might appear interesting to an open-minded person, given our limited time and energy with full-time jobs and other family and community responsibilities, we had to measure carefully both the amount of energy we could afford to part with, and to what degree we were willing to invest ourselves. I felt that by understanding our personal purpose while on this earth, the knowledge could help guide our choices and help us make better decisions for our well-being.

Well, it would appear that Sue's friend took this as a personal challenge of some kind, which I suppose it was for each of us. Her immediate challenge back to me was, "Do you know what your purpose is?" spoken in a tone of voice like, "Aha, I got you there!" And without a moment's hesitation, I responded that my purpose was to create things of beauty. This statement took me by surprise as much as it did her! She had nothing further to add following several moments of dead silence. I could feel the electricity in the air. The conversation moved to a different, safer topic.

I might have inadvertently stepped on this woman's spiritual toes. Clearly, she didn't expect that any of us would know our life's purpose, and that it was absurd to suggest that we should. After all, don't most people go around asking that "purpose" question their whole life, seldom finding a satisfactory answer?

In fact, while I had been thinking a lot about what my life's mission might be, I hadn't yet landed on a firm answer other than getting myself solidly healed from depression. I had been tinkering with the notion that perhaps I was put on this earth to support people who were struggling with depression. But that's not the answer that popped into my head. It was *to create things of beauty*! Who knew?

I experienced the positive effect that being around beauty had on my own mood, but I hadn't really thought about beauty outside of that. Truth is, I hadn't been thinking about much of anything outside of getting well and staying well. So the statement really took me by surprise. But I am sticking with it, because I like the idea of being here to create all the beautiful things I want in whatever materials speak to me. I like the idea that what I make from fabrics, fiber, threads, yarns, leather, and fur does not need to be functional, that it can be for its own sake and nothing more. I *really* like that idea, because it expands the possibilities in all directions when the thing need serve no other purpose other than to give joy—first to me, and if others can take joy from my work as well, all the better.

Oh, how Spirit finds interesting ways of working within us.

• • • EXERCISE • • •

Learn to Focus

Here is how I enter the sensing mode for identifying what I call "emotional junk," or negative emotions that ego hangs on to for no apparent, useful purpose other than out of habit. Remember, ego's specialty is guarding what already exists. These instructions were adapted from the Focusing Institute website, www.focusing.org. Try this and check out the website if you find it helps.

Sit in a quiet place where you will be undisturbed for twenty minutes or more. Close your eyes and take a deep, relaxed breath, exhaling slowly. Do this three times or more until you begin to feel connected with your breath. Using your mind and solar plexus (that area below the breastbone and above the stomach) try to identify the issue or thing that you want to sense more about. Perhaps it is a recent event that really bothers you; perhaps the event triggered an unfortunate memory.

Go into that thing or memory, as if you were in meditation. Keep focused not *on* that place but *in* it, deeper and deeper until you begin to feel an emotion from it. At first, you may not know where the emotion is coming from; it may suddenly make itself felt, like out of the blue, or it might be obvious and strong. Pay attention to it; ask it what it is, what it represents, what it wants, why it is here. Avoid the temptation to judge it. Try to put a name to it: "You feel like... sadness, hurt, anger..." Once you have attached a label to it, ask it if that is right. Does it feel like you have figured out what it is about? There's a good chance that the word doesn't quite capture the emotion exactly. It might capture some of it but not all of it. Begin asking it what else it is, what more does it have to say? Another word or series of words might come to you, and perhaps this feels like you are getting closer to the core of the matter.

Continue with this internal probing exercise until you feel you have pinpointed the issue as closely as you can. You will know you've hit the bull's-eye when you feel a shift in your felt sense. It can feel like something that has clicked into the right gear. If the felt sense could make a noise, it would be a definite clunking sound. And once that shift takes place, your sense of it will feel rock solid. Bingo. You can test it by trying on a slightly different label, but the likelihood is that it will reject it for the previous one; you will then know for sure that it's right.

Now, you can say to yourself that this negativity concerning this or that is really about such and such, and my pain body (or ego) was using it to protect me in some way.

This is where you can have a heart-to-heart conversation with your loving ego, perhaps as a journal entry, thanking her for wanting to protect you. Tell her how much you appreciate her looking out for you all these years. And now that you understand better where the fear (or hurt, or sorrow) is coming from, you can promise her that you are okay with the situation in question and that there is no need to fear any longer.

This exercise has helped me to release untold emotional baggage whose only purpose was to clutter my emotions, create artificial limitations, and confuse me, and served to contract rather than expand my world.

Having cleared the bigger chunks of emotion held in the body, I find myself using a shortened version of the technique to check in with my body's felt sense, in response to specific occurrences or opportunities in my daily life. I find it is a neat tool that is worthwhile practicing and getting better at.

I've heard people say that they don't feel connected with their body, that they mostly experience life in their heads. A focusing technique like this one can help develop a better balance with body, mind, and spirit. It's uncanny how much information is stored in the body, and with practice, it is possible to unlock that knowledge and to tap into the body's intelligence.

The expensive course I mentioned in chapter one was called "Integral Enlightenment: Evolving beyond Ego" by Craig Hamilton. It was a live, web-based, nine-week course. And it was this transaction that cemented my partnership with Divine Spirit and that led me to experience lasting wellness.

I wanted to "contribute to the evolutionary progress of the collective momentum"; I wanted to be an expression of my best self aligning with a divine pool of like-minded souls.

I was a teenager when I first ran into the notion of ego. I had joined a group to explore the existence of spirit guides and to learn how to communicate with them and the spirit realm. My seventeen-year-old mind recalls that ego had a bad reputation, and above all, it was not to be trusted. I learned a little more about ego in my Psychology 101 class in university. But I never understood ego quite as clearly until Craig Hamilton explained it in this course.

Now I see that ego is not such a bad kid; she's just defending the reality that she's always known. And she wants to be heard, just like everyone else. She wants the airtime that is her due. After all, ego works hard at protecting us. So I think she deserves a break! (That doesn't mean that I will allow her to be in charge of me, though.)

Participants were asked to answer ten questions from the point of view of "evolutionary impulse," that which observes and desires a greater goodness and truth.

As I am inside this impulse...

1. What excites me is...
2. My purpose is...
3. What I want is...
4. What I am most passionate about is...
5. What I have no patience for is...
6. My nature is...
7. In my human form, how do I feel about the limitations of body, mind, needs, concerns, etc. of [your name]?
8. What does a life look like when I am the driving force?
9. What's the highest game I can play in this form?
10. What would I do differently with this life up to this point?

As part of the course, I had the opportunity to participate in group meditations with thousands of people from around the world connected by telephone and computer. This was powerful.

I learned to tell the difference between evolutionary impulse and guidance from ego. I learned about purity of motive (or drive) and why I need not care about outcomes. What freedom this brought me!

I learned how to let go of preference, to surrender the needs, wants, and concerns of the narrow self. I learned to let go of old stories about myself, of everything I was convinced I knew about others or myself. This was about opening the whole self— with Spirit in the lead—to a new way of thinking, being, loving, giving, of putting "out there" for the greater good, without expectation or return on investment and with purity of motive.

Ah... this relaxed my whole being—my mind, my muscles, my shoulders, and my heart. And it lit up my creative joy!

In one of the lessons, I was to reflect and write down ten statements about myself:

1. I love solitude and meditation.
2. I value my relationship with God most of all.
3. I am self-motivated and determined.
4. I am creative, intuitive, and bright.
5. I love young children.
6. I am drawn to prayer, the rosary, and contemplation.
7. I like some structure in my life.
8. I enjoy helping others (particularly guiding them to help themselves).
9. I am an authentic person and I seek authenticity in others.
10. I enjoy travel, especially when connecting with people from all walks of life.

I learned about the three parts of the self—ego, higher self, and authentic self—and that each part has a different perception and experience of life. Understanding and recognizing these dimensions within ourselves enables and empowers us to choose the perception that works best for us, to decide which part of us we will align with.

I learned that a fully "evolved" person reaches a point where the only acceptable choice at all is where there is no real choice to make, because the alternative to choosing what leads to the greater good is not acceptable to you any longer. That it is a matter of tapping into your will to consistently make this choice even when you don't feel like it, perhaps when there is fear.

The thinking was that most people who are on a spiritual path are not in it for big enough reasons, that the motivation to stay on the path, no matter what, needs to be larger. I learned about radical authenticity, the idea of being comfortable with transparency and open communication. I love the notion of radical authenticity! (This connects with Brené Brown's notion that inviting vulnerability is key to love and happiness.)

I learned what a moral force can do when positioned at the center of your life, of the inherent beauty of a heartfelt connection to the Source, especially a connection that is shared with thousands of like-minded souls across the globe.

I learned about the four spheres of the evolutionary self and the motivation centers:

1. Awakening to our interdependence
Everything I do impacts the whole, all the time.

2. Awakening to the evolutionary imperative
We have such potential as a human race to be good, to do good, to care for one another, to share in the earth's wealth. Making the choices and actions that shape the future in this direction is what's important. My life, as a contribution to this picture, is pretty important, isn't it?

3. Relating to life from God's point of view
Isn't *that* an interesting mind shift—to see our lives as a sacred call to manifest divinity in all its forms, to concern ourselves with the highest good imaginable? Let it be God's will, not my will. Let *thy* will be done (from the Lord's Prayer, Matthew 6:9–13). Most important of all is to be worthy of God's company. This is an easy one to remember for our day-to-day living, and perhaps not so easy to do but an awesome intention.

4. Applying the Deathbed Perspective (for a deeper order of integrity)

What was this life for? What were the most important moments and why? To what degree has my life been an expression of my highest truth and understanding? Did I consistently do the right thing when it mattered most? What are my regrets?

The idea is to stare this choice in the face every day and to face our own motivation when we don't choose the higher good.

The single most important thing I got from this course was learning how I could go about changing my mindset, that my thoughts were choices that I made, not something that was hard and fast and forever ingrained in my bones.

When I took this course, I was being treated by two doctors: my family doctor, a man who has been practicing medicine for nearly forty years, and a second physician also with loads of experience, especially in treating patients with depression and anxiety. Both of these respected caregivers told me I needed to change my thinking if I hoped to return to work successfully. ("Michèle, you need to change your attitude, because you will never change the organization.")

Neither provided a how-to guide for achieving this change, though. I was left with figuring out how one goes about flipping her lifelong thoughts upside down and backward. After all, didn't my thinking define the person I was?

Hmm, maybe not.

A Word about Medication

Even with the new skills I and the better coping strategies I was developing, it still took all of my power to keep the darkness at bay, and as in most things, some days were better than others. I could no more predict what temperature *the mood* would be on any particular day, or even hour by hour, than I could believe

the darkness would ever be gone for good. That lack of predictability in itself was a heavy load to bear, not only for me but

for those close to me, especially
for my husband who was called
to live with the unpredictability of
the mood day in and day out. Not
knowing whether my mood would
be okay or in the dungeon—a
good or elevated mood was often
a short-lived occurrence—meant
that I avoided making plans that
involved others, whether family,
friends, or discretionary appointments like a haircut or going to the
bank. This not-knowing was one
of the hardest things to live with.

"Overcoming loneli-
ness and moving to
connection… is not
merely an exercise
in pop psychology
fulfillment or personal
gratification. It is the
very goal of exis-
tence, of being and
of becoming. It is
what our soul prints
seek."—Marc Gafni

My life had become one-dimensional and linear. I desperately
needed to get back some depth, especially in an expanding sense.

My friends understood that my spur-of-the-moment calls to
get together were fueled by an all-too-rare positive mood, and
that when I was out of touch for a time, it meant only that
my mood prevented me from connecting. My siblings, most
of whom lived several hours away, were generally unaware of
my internal battles, but my children, who were now adults,
understood.

It's hard if not impossible for someone to comprehend the
struggle unless they have been preconditioned through personal
exposure to depression and anxiety, either through their own
experience or that of a close friend or relative. Otherwise, most

people just don't get it. And it's not typically something that can be made clear through one conversation. It takes a huge commitment for someone outside to listen to numerous monologues about what it's like to be inside depression. Our society is slowly becoming more aware of this illness, at least at a theoretical level. But we are still far from understanding depression or the person experiencing it. So I have stopped trying to explain, except to an intimate few when they ask.

I can't imagine what it must have been like for my husband to live with second-hand depression in full bloom. The stress and worry must have been constant for him. Unlike during my first experience of depression in 2002, which was deeper and darker and more difficult for me to voice my experience, this time around, in 2009, I openly communicated with Robert about the illness and he actively listened. I kept him abreast of my progress by sharing my therapist's feedback and my own sense of development.

All the same, I was often not in control of my mood and emotions because after all, I was living inside the depression. My thinking was foggy and disconnected. And I could never let go of the control I was forced to exert on my mind, because if I did, my automatic thinking would right away seek its natural course: negativity and darkness. I lived in a constant state of being on guard, which makes it hard to relax.

I continued to work every day and every hour at directing my thoughts in a positive, forward direction. Without my constant watchfulness over my thinking, I could revert to old thought patterns, which acted like dead weight dragging my whole self into a downward spiral. That is how my head worked. That is, until I starting taking the right medication for me (Cymbalta).

I was not fond of the term "mental illness" as my good husband can attest. I remember well my first encounter with the term being used in reference to me. It was the day following Robert's dear friend's out-of-town wedding, at which Robert was best man. In this role, he was expected not only to attend to the groom prior to the ceremony but also to sit at the head table without me, a decision that was unknown to him until the afternoon of the wedding.

I had spent the day by myself in a nearby park while Robert visited with the groom and engaged in best-man stuff. Having spent hours entertaining myself by reading and people-watching, I looked forward to the comfort of being with my husband again. He was my anchor. He was also the only person I knew at the wedding other than the bride and groom.

I met him at the reception hall where both the ceremony and the dinner were being held. That's when Robert told me we would not be sitting together. And that's when it happened.

Everything around me began to move in slow motion. People milling about and chitchatting were in a fog as my mind veered into panic mode and froze. I felt vulnerable and defenseless. Here I stood utterly ill-equipped to fend for myself in a room full of strangers and a few acquaintances, expected to go through the social motions when I had just been dealt quite a blow.

I felt wide-eyed and scared like a deer caught in headlights; I was experiencing another implosion. I lashed out at Robert in my quiet, rigid, and cool manner, because I suddenly found myself without my only protection and protector.

When it came time to sit down for the meal, Robert was already seated and I had no idea what to do next. I would have given anything to vanish through the floor and be gone. I didn't know how to choose a place to sit! I saw that guests were joining friends and family at their tables. But I knew no one. How was I expected to know where to sit, given my depleted condition? Talk about feeling awkward and out of place! I kept looking around searching for any clue to help me move from the spot in the middle of the room where I was glued, as people moved around me to find their tables. I have no idea how long I stood frozen, but it felt like forever to me.

The groom eventually came to my rescue and I was led to a half-empty table of singles, all decades younger than me. I felt wretched, like the dregs of society, rejected, dejected, banished. I had no business being there. All through dinner and the usual speeches, I prayed to be freed from this achingly uncomfortable ordeal. As dinner finally concluded and the hall was being made ready for dancing, I made a beeline for the exit.

I was finally alone and immediately felt safer. I took a long walk, high heels and all, which eventually calmed my nerves. But returning to the reception following my forty-minute walk was out of the question. I could no more face all those people than I could have delivered a valedictorian address to an expectant crowd of thousands. As it was nearing dusk by then, I unobtrusively changed into my jeans behind some bushes in the parking lot and waited in the car for Robert so we could finally drive the two hours home.

It was a terrifying experience. And it was not a pleasant one for Robert, who found himself without a date for no apparent reason. He eventually figured out that I had left but didn't know why or where I had gone. I did feel bad for not telling him, but there was no way I could force myself back into that hall. A part of me also felt angry at him for having abandoned me, which was not logical, of course, but try explaining that to a panicked and frightened mind.

I later learned that I had experienced social anxiety. I hadn't known how vulnerable I was until I observed my own response to an unfortunate situation, when frozen fear overtook my body and my brain. In fact, the day before leaving to go to the wedding, Robert and I had discussed whether I should attend, not knowing if I was well enough. I wanted to be there for Robert and for his friend, whom I knew quite well. In the end, I felt it would be all right since Robert would be with me.

> "Joy, like honor and serenity and so much else we ache and sweat for, is only available to us when we actively seek something else instead."
> —Marc Gafni

The following day, Robert asked if we could talk about what had taken place the previous evening. I wanted to explain things as well, and I was surprised that he was the one to approach me, as it was out of character for him to initiate a discussion of this nature.

He wanted to understand what had happened, but mostly, he expressed his concern for me and thought I should reconsider my decision not to take medication. At the very least, he wanted me to discuss the options with my doctor. That's when I heard the words that caused me to bite his head off: "mental illness."

The exchange went something like this:

Robert: Given your experience at the wedding, do you think it's time to talk with your doctor about taking medication?

Michèle: But you know how I feel about taking drugs. And they don't work for me anyway. And I'm managing things with

CBT. I've worked hard at it for a year and I think I am doing much better.

Robert: I think you might need treatment that goes beyond talk therapy for your mental illness.

Michèle: I do not have a mental illness! *(I said with a raised and excitable voice.)*

Robert: What is it that you have, then?

Michèle: I have a mental "condition."

Robert: Call it whatever you want, but it is affecting your quality of life in a big way. It's affecting *our* quality of life.

I agreed on the later point, but I was not prepared to concede on taking medication. My mind was fixed against taking drugs due to my earlier experience with unacceptable and long-lasting side effects. It took a few days more for me to reopen that conversation with Robert and tell him I was ready to see my doctors about the options.

I first consulted my CBT therapist. I expected her to share my concerns regarding my taking medication. Instead, I was surprised by her strong encouragement of the idea. She believed that although I was doing well in managing my thoughts, I would need the extra help medication could provide when I returned to work. She said it would make what I had learned with CBT easier to execute and that it would give me a fighting chance at having a better life. The idea now appealed to me if it meant less continual fighting with my thoughts.

My family doctor, as it turned out, was just as eager for me to try medication again; he prescribed a new drug that hadn't been available when I was last in the market seven years prior. Although I was encouraged by the newness of the medication, and presumably more advanced science, I still had strong reservations due to the potential, dreaded side effects.

However, I felt I no longer had a choice, not only because of Robert's concerns but because I was tired of being a slave to *the mood*; it was managing me when it should be the one being managed.

I started feeling the positive effects within a few weeks of taking Cymbalta. I was feeling better, which slowly grew into feeling fantastic! I hadn't felt that good since I was a kid. It was as if the world had finally turned on a light in my direction. I couldn't help having a permanent smile on my face. I felt fully alive with my senses on super alert. I was thrilled to be alive like a baby enjoying the wonder of breathing and seeing her mama's smiling face over her crib.

I had loads of energy and wanted to do everything that came my way. I was fully engaged in life and happy for the first time in twenty years. What a feeling to experience life to the fullest, like a brand new person. What a trip to not be afraid to go outside and talk to people. Quite the contrast from my natural, before-drug state!

I was back at work and thrilled to be functional and productive, to be engaged, and to have a salary; I was part of the world again and I was high on life! (And a little high on the drug, I would later conclude.)

I did experience side effects similar to those of seven years prior, especially teeth-grinding and jaw-clenching, not only during the night but throughout the day as well. *Oh no, not this again!* I thought. Luckily, a second medication eliminated eighty-five percent of the grinding, and I decided I could live with the leftover clenching although my teeth complained from the load.

The medication and I got along well for about two years, at which point I experienced a sudden episode of severe anxiety lasting several hours, over nothing I could put my finger on and everything in general. As far as I could tell, this "event" had come out of the great blue sky and without plausible explanation. Yikes! I had no idea what was going on, but it scared me.

I immediately discussed the episode with my manager and made an appointment to see my doctor and was prescribed a third drug (Remeron). I knew this one could have some significant side effects and I was not mistaken. For me, this included heavy morning fog of the brain, lasting four to five hours, and significant weight gain.

I had to be absent from work in the mornings because I could not think through or understand even mildly complex thoughts. I eventually learned to manage this side effect by changing the time at which I took the medication, moving it to the dinner hour rather than bedtime. But because the drug made me feel very hungry, that meant I had the whole evening to eat, raiding cupboards like a depraved creature; my stomach felt like it was starving, hunger pains and all. It was pretty weird that within twenty minutes of finishing our evening meal, I would start looking for something to eat, anything I could put my hands on, even stale soda crackers.

I gained twenty-five pounds in the first six to eight months. This was the first time in my life that I carried extra weight, and I didn't like it one bit. I still have the weight on and I like it no better. I finally reached a compromise time for taking this drug, settling on 7:30 p.m., which means I still snack too much in the evening, but luckily my early bedtime limits the amount of food intake. (And there's no food allowed in bed!)

I later learned that it is not unusual for a drug to lose some of its effectiveness after a time. (Gee, there goes my newfound confidence in medication.) But I have never felt so good about myself or about life, and that is thanks in the main to medication.

> "How does knowing your uniqueness conquer your loneliness? You will not be lonely because you will be in relationship with yourself."
> —Marc Gafni

In 2002 when I experienced my first episode of severe depression, I was prescribed a number of medications in four- to six-week intervals, but none worked for me. Each drug carried a worse side effect than the last, from nightly nightmares to insomnia, drowsiness, headaches, and finally, severe involuntary tremors.

I was advised by a neurologist, to whom I was referred for the tremors, to stop taking Sebelium (which I had been taking for one year to prevent my all-too-frequent migraines) because depression was a potential side effect (along with anxiety, insomnia, lack of appetite, and nightmares—all of which I was experiencing). Four months after stopping this drug, the depression began to lift. I started enjoying nature walks and I picked up my knitting again.

After months of living with the shaking in my hands, legs and jaw, my teeth chattering as if I were freezing cold (a condition that remained for a year after being taken off all medication), and the thought that a medication might have been responsible for sending me into this terrible depression to begin with,

I wanted no part of taking any more drugs. My doctors knew this and accepted it as a necessary constraint for my treatment.

And while my family doctor supported my decision, he offered no alternative avenues to explore for dealing with the depression.

LETTING GO

"Anytime you are filled with resentment, you're turning the controls of your emotional life over to others to manipulate."—Wayne Dyer

In preparing for my return to work, my biggest challenge turned out to be letting go. Letting go of fear, resentment, anger, frustration, blame, and mistrust. These were some powerful emotions that I needed to let go of if I hoped to return to, and be safe in, the very environment that kept triggering my depression.

There is such futility in hanging on to these big feelings. What purpose does it serve except to keep me drowning in negative emotion? It does nothing to improve my situation—quite the contrary. It does not make me happy, only bitter. Yet, I hang on to them tightly.

Letting go is something I had to learn. And it turned out to be the most important learning, because it was the very thing that set in motion the true healing process.

Without the freedom from emotional pain that letting go provides, I could not heal and grow from the experience. I was held back as if stuck in the muck. And if I was going through some heavy muck, the least I should be allowed to expect is to learn from it, no?

One of the most important lessons was that no matter how vindicated I might have felt, I needed to consider the damage that holding on to resentment and anger was doing, and to whom. The real damage was certainly not to them (the organization where I worked). No matter how strongly I hung on to my feelings, it wouldn't change the facts. "They" probably would never even learn of the crazy-making frustration they had caused. It was an organization after all, not one particular individual who was responsible. It was unreasonable of me to expect an organization to admit the wrong done and to ask for my forgiveness. Let's be real!

The real damage was being done to me, and only to me.

Was I okay with sustaining that heavy story? Or did I wish to be rid of the junk? I chose to be done with it.

It was a vital shift in my thinking, a conscious decision to release my hold on those feelings, so I could keep on moving and growing in my authenticity. Jon Kabat-Zinn describes that inner shift as being "akin to letting your palm open to unhand something you have been holding on to."

At first, the idea of letting go of the frustration I had toward my workplace felt like I was giving in. When I told my therapist this, she corrected my thinking. "Letting go does not mean you are giving in," she said. "It means that you are moving on." Ah! Now, that I could accept! Because I sure did want to move on. But I wanted to do it in a way that was authentic to my emerging self. I did not want to compromise on that part.

I found that by letting go and moving on, I was able to open up to a whole new world, one that allowed me to view my work as play and offered opportunities for growing new skills. I enjoyed developing skills that my authentic self really wanted to learn for becoming a better web editor and assisting my colleagues with their online needs. It felt productive and useful.

Get this: Letting go allowed me to *flourish* in the workplace. The same organization that previously had crushed me now provided opportunities for me to grow in areas that I was passionate about—clear communication and creativity. As the new web editor for our branch website, I was able to combine these two components in a most delightful way. And it (the organization) hadn't changed a thing!

If this Spirit-led transformation had not taken place, I would not be telling this story.

I did a lot of visualization to make this healthy workplace happen for myself. From all I had been learning, I understood that the first step to success was to actively imagine the reality that I wanted, then to trust that Spirit would orchestrate the rest.

I know of a colleague who is stuck in a similar resentment of the same organization, based on years of frustration at having been refused the necessary accommodation for her mobility limitation. She was forced to leave her job to barely subsist on insurance payments in lieu of a paycheck, causing her to use up her savings to supplement her living over several years.

When she eventually returned to her job, she was given the accommodation she originally had requested, which makes it possible for her to perform the work. Understandably, she is angry at the organization for withholding the accommodation for so long. She holds it responsible for depleting her savings and having to remortgage her home.

I feel bad for her and her circumstances, and agree that it seems unfair. But I also know that no matter how long she stays angry, whether she voices that anger or not, the organization probably will not be asking her forgiveness, nor will it take responsibility for the damage. The organization's primary concern is meeting production targets, even if that means "inconveniencing" an employee. They probably followed the human resources rules as tightly as they could and would have nothing further to explain. Unfortunate, but true.

It's not hard to imagine who is more likely to lose such a battle—the vulnerable individual or the large organization. This doesn't mean the damage done was not real. It certainly was. But the wiser choice might still be letting go and moving on. I wish her every success in this difficult yet worthwhile undertaking.

SOUL PRINTS

Another great resource in my journey to wellness was Marc Gafni's *Soul Prints: Your Path to Fulfillment*. His work helped me learn to liberate myself from the unresolved issues that were "jamming my frequencies" and preventing me from picking up on my own true calling. Perhaps this is what the notion of getting out of your own way is?

He explained that our "soul print" seeks to reach out to the prints of other souls—to touch them, and to be touched by them in turn. The more our soul prints connect, the sharper their signatures, and the more sustained and expansive our souls will be.

• • • Exercises • • •

Your Cup of Elijah

The Cup of Elijah is not for sale! It represents your highest self and your core integrity, your deepest self, when all other layers and postures are removed. The Cup of Elijah is about your most personal hopes and dreams. It is about believing in miracles, dreaming the impossible, about reaching beyond your grasp to find your heaven. Here are the three critical questions to ask yourself. I've provided my own answers below.

What is your Cup of Elijah?

1. What about yourself would you *never* give up?
2. What do you wish you had more of?
3. What three material items in your life would you not sell, ever?

What would I never give up?

- My creativity
- My Francophone-ness
- My passion and *joie de vivre*
- My love and respect for my children
- My love for my siblings and my mom
- My authenticity and drive for it
- My integrity and humility
- My love of reading and self-improvement

What do I wish I had more of?

- Laughter
- Good friends
- Headache-free days
- Time spent with Robert at Twin Peaks (our cabin)
- Hikes in the woods

What material items would I never sell?
- My sewing machines and tools
- My family photos
- My wedding band, fifteenth anniversary ring, Citizen watch, and string of pearls from Robert
- The ring I designed in honor of my two engineer kids
- My black Dutch Oven pot
- My sister Anne's paintings

Yes Questions

List ten questions for yourself for which you absolutely know the answer is a resounding yes. Ask yourself the questions and answer them with feeling, out loud.

Here is my list of "yes" things:

1. Do you love starting the day with a hot cup of yerba maté? Yes!
2. Do you love Felix, your cuddly baby grandson? Yes!
3. Do you enjoy going to your local bookstore and finding that the very book you were looking for is now half price? Yes!
4. Do you love spinning on your wheel on the porch of down-home's farmhouse? Yes! And outside at your cabin when there are no bugs? Yes!
5. Do you like going to Twin Peaks in the winter for a snowshoe in the woods? Yes! Especially with Robert? Yes!
6. Do you enjoy the sound of Robert lighting the wood stove in the early morning, while you lounge in bed? Yes!
7. Do you love touching and handling luscious fabric? Yes!
8. Do you love beautiful, functional hardware and fixtures? Yes!
9. Do you like climbing into a freshly made bed with sheets from the clothesline? Yes!

10. Did you enjoy your Peruvian Spanish teacher, Cristina? Yes! Enjoy the vibration of *yes*, which automatically raises your energetic vibration.

MY FAVORITE THING IS...

As an alternate to the Yes Questions, you can list ten of your favorite things or situations that you love; start the sentence with "My favorite thing is..." or "I love it when..."

AFFIRMATIONS

I learned that belief is at the root of what I create. I wrote about my beliefs in my journal and talked about them with my "believing eyes."

I also wrote affirmations:

I believe in the power of me.

I believe I can. I am.

I believe in my happiness.

I believe in the need to mark my progress.

I believe in the power of us (me and Spirit).

I believe it, just because.

I learned to set intentions and charge them with emotion so that they could resonate out there in the world of energy. Every morning, I would set my most important intention for the day, sometimes surprising myself with what my soul voiced back to me.

DIGGING FOR GOLD

One of Sonia Choquette's exercises is called Digging for Gold: With no advance thinking, ask yourself out loud, "If I wasn't afraid, I would..." and fill in the blank.

I learned the importance of connecting with others, because as Sonia says, no one creates alone. As a natural loner, I had to consciously work at this. I learned that the more a person expresses her support of and for others, the more that emotion is reflected back at you. I learned of the importance of surrounding myself with supportive energy.

I trained myself to laugh as much as possible, because laughter raises our vibrations and can accelerate the creation process. I watched YouTube videos of babies laughing (because, honestly, who can resist laughing babies?).

The "Creating Your Heart's Desire" course taught me to develop a habit of noting what Choquette calls "psychic hits," noticing when my intuition was right on, like when my inner voice warned me of a traffic jam up ahead, or gave me a feeling that I had left something behind, or when it led me to the perfect find at my favorite thrift store.

I learned to state these psychic hits out loud so that Spirit would know I had received the message. I also would tell receptive friends about them to show the universe I appreciated the effort. As suggested, I started writing them down on a small pad that I carried in my handbag. It surprised me how often these hits would happen; it seemed the more my awareness of synchronicity increased, the more these mini-occurrences grew in frequency. I believe our attention and magnetic energy pull them in the more we pay them mind and respect them.

MY AFFIRMATIONS

For Life in General

- I am courage, I am faith, I am inspired.
- I live my personal beliefs through inspired action and shine my light brightly.
- I gratefully allow guidance and inspiration to flow through me.

- I am wanted and loved; I am worthy.
- I come from greatness; I attract greatness; I am greatness.
- I fully trust that others know what is best for them.
- I give my joy to others, and this helps them in some way.
- I integrate stillness into each day.
- My home is filled with positive, giving energy; my friends enjoy coming here.
- I am focused and determined; I am clear in my goals and resolve.
- I can handle most anything one thing at a time; that's the way all people do things, one at a time.
- I give of myself to others; I serve in God's purpose.
- I have the power to handle challenges presented to me and transform them into strength and learning. Even though I had no power as a child, I have great inner strength today, which comes from my intuition, self-knowledge, gentleness, and good energy flow.
- I am a calm, delightful woman with an inner spark, who enjoys giving of herself.
- I balance my enthusiasm for good work with inner calm and self-care.
- I look outside myself now, and connect with others; this contributes to my health.
- I don't ruminate on negative things; I pay attention to the wonderful things in my life, and I am grateful.
- I attract only peace into my world; I live joyfully and am accompanied by other joyful spirits.
- When faced with difficulties, I seek a middle ground.
- I set myself above my emotions.

- My spirit glows with purity, clarity, goodness, love, devotion, promise, achievement, and service.
- I am poised and centered regardless of what goes before me.
- I live with fluidity and I trust my inner self; I enjoy the uncertainty because of the newness it offers.

For Going Back to Work
- I am engaged in productive and safe-for-me work.
- I enjoy a balanced life.
- I allow joy to be part of my work life.
- I intend to land in a good job that I like, with a good manager who is strong, a good person and who knows how to manage people.

I have...
- strength to go back to work
- stamina to be stronger than the negative thoughts
- mental discipline to stay in charge

I have Spirit's healing...
- to keep depression at bay
- to allow joy to come through
- for my talents to breathe
- for my essence to stay alive

For at least twenty consecutive days, I repeat...
- Spirit encourages my truest self to bloom.
- I know my own voice now—I am guided to use it in a strong and gentle way.
- I am mentally strong, energetic, and inspired.
- As I return to work, I enjoy being and feeling productive; I ask my Admiral guide to help me.

• I am responsible for identifying and communicating my needs and limitations; this will help me to feel safe.

The name "Admiral" makes reference to a dream I had during this period, in which appeared a man wearing a light blue uniform with gold bars on the epaulets, similar in appearance to the Canadian Air Force's uniform. He got my attention by exuding a very strong presence and inspiring my confidence in him, and he seemed to be leading me. I felt a strong bond with him, not as a lover or a father but as a wise friend and mentor whom I had known for most of my life, and whom I trusted completely. I felt safe in his presence and unworried (unlike how I felt when I was awake and in the real world). I feel that he was a spirit guide to me and I named him Admiral. I haven't seen him since, not in the uniform anyway, but I believe he is still around and watches over me. I love his presence. He makes me feel completely safe.

. . . .

"Creativity is intelligence having fun."—Albert Einstein

. . . .

Who would have thought creativity would play such an important role in my get-well plan? Although making stuff had been a part of my life since childhood, my illness taught me that creative expression was vital for my soul, and that when making things—whether they turned out beautiful, experimental, and for my eyes only, or ordinary and practical— the result was less important than the creative act itself.

Engaging in creativity did something to my brain that I didn't understand but knew I wanted more of: it introduced a good feeling and sense of well-being. There was a moment of realization when I understood that being creative was no longer a niceto-do-when-time-permits thing but rather had become a mustdo-for-my-sanity kind of thing. The simple act of creating set my brain on a healthy path, contributed to my overall health, and was essential to keeping me feeling good.

Just as my daily routine started with the act of connecting with Spirit, I needed to give creativity a central place somewhere in my day.

To kick-start this change (and to convince my subconscious that I was serious about it, that creativity was to get equal air time as did the rest of me), I decided to spend time in my sewing/ craft room every day (I called it my "Joy Room"), whether I felt inspired or not, whether I was motivated or not, even if for just a short time (at least thirty minutes). This was now a part of my discipline for getting back to good mental health.

> "When you become comfortable with uncertainty, infinite possibilities open up in your life... If uncertainty is unacceptable to you, it turns into fear. If it is perfectly acceptable, it turns into increased aliveness, alertness and creativity."
> —Eckhart Tolle

Knowing that I *needed* creativity as a regular part of my life felt fantastic.

And I now had one more concrete daily activity to include in my get-well plan.

This was well and good while at home on medical leave, but what would happen to my resolve once I was back at work? Especially in a large organization that I felt wouldn't know creativity if it hit it between the eyes? How would I figure this one out?

I did it with the help of visualization. I delved into my body's inner knowing and was able to observe within myself what I needed to attain better job satisfaction: to feel productive while on the job. I knew that if I could dip into my creative talent and make a product that was of use to someone, regardless of what it was, this would satisfy my need.

This might sound obvious to some, but it hadn't been obvious to me these past twenty years in my job.

"Here's a thought," I said to myself. "What if I switched my focus away from working on issues that felt like lost causes?" In my workspace, I began to keep an eye open for any creative work that flowed *with* the current of the organization rather than against it.

This calls for some background. In 1991 when I first joined the organization, I was hired to coordinate and monitor delivery of French Language Services to the province's Francophone minority, who numbered only 6 percent of Ontario's 13 million people and were not vocal in claiming those services. It was a hard sell to justify improving services when those clients were as good as invisible. Not surprisingly, and especially given ongoing cutbacks, my organization didn't see the value in dedicating scarce resources for services that were barely used. Francophones rarely asked for services in French, to which they were legally entitled, partly because the expectation—based on their prior experience—was that these were second-rate services not up to the standard of similar English services. Who could blame them? It was an awkward, no-win situation across most areas of the province designated to provide services in French—a real catch-22.

I held this job for ten years, and while I believed in the cause with all my heart, I became quite drained and tired of the isolation by virtue of being the sole person doing this work in a decentralized organization numbering around 3,500 people. I felt alone in the fight and I didn't have the drive for it anymore.

My second job involved monitoring service standards across the same ministry and across all programs. I was to guide managers in developing their own program-specific standards for improving customer service. This, in an organization that for years had been downsizing and closing down offices— another no-win situation. On top of that, the job was huge and should have been staffed with three people, not one (they later hired two more employees).

It was five months into this new job that I felt like I had run headfirst into a brick wall and fell apart in the office of my former manager, Arthur. Lucky for me, he knew what to do. His call to the professionals at EAP got me through that first panic.

Looking from the outside in, it's no surprise that a decade spent working against the grain of the organization would lead me to an eventual breakdown. That type of work did not mesh with my temperament, but I didn't know it at the time.

But, I had a new focus now. I would latch on to work that was mainstream, and I didn't much care what the topic was as long as I could feel productive. Brilliant!

I would no longer be called on to influence people to accomplish my program's objectives; I would not provide organizational leadership and be expected to convince executives to adopt "my" cause. In the new environment that I was envisioning, they would be the ones guiding the boat along their stream; I would simply jump on board and provide my creative and writing abilities. *Wouldn't that be sweet,* I thought.

I imagined how wonderful it would be to have a job that involved creativity. From reading Eckhart Tolle's *A New Earth: Awakening to Your Life's Purpose,* with a premise that life is exactly what you make it, no more and no less, and actively practicing law-of-attraction principles, I started to believe that it was possible for me to attract the kind of work that was good for me.

If I could apply the techniques I was learning from Sonia Choquette's online course, which puts forward analogous principles, couldn't I engage in a similar approach for manifesting my kind of work? What did I have to lose? I started practicing even before returning to work, just to see what might happen.

I began by preparing my mind, picturing myself in an office cubicle, sitting at a computer, doing creative tasks. I imagined the colors on my monitor, moving lines about, just playing with the colors, really. While I was at it, I also imagined that my work was highly valued by others.

I did this while I was still on leave, and in a more focused way, while I waited for my manager to coordinate my return to work, which took too many weeks.

Next, I enlisted the help of divine intervention to put me in the right place for attracting such work.

As good fortune would have it, once back at work the first project I was assigned—at my suggestion and as part of the work-hardening process—was to create a participant's manual for a diversity mentoring program that my department was preparing to launch.

Delighted with the opportunity, I approached the work like a game, designing attractive page layouts on my computer, exploring the use of new software, which I quite enjoyed, selecting and positioning text and images in a way that was pleasing to the eye, and working with lots of color! I absolutely loved the work and I successfully met my deadline.

The project was recognized as a high-quality product, not only by the content experts but, more important to me, by the participants themselves. Other organizations began requesting a copy of my sixty-page manual so they could adapt it for their own use. I was, of course, very pleased to share my work.

This was the most rewarding work I had ever done. Having spent twenty years doing what I finally realized had been the wrong type of work, I now knew what doing good work actually felt like. And I knew from the depth of my soul that I wanted and needed more of this.

"The greater danger for most of us lies not in setting our aim too high and falling short; but in setting our aim too low, and achieving our mark."
—Michelangelo

I gave myself permission to seek more of this type of work that was better suited to my skills and temperament, even if it meant taking a cut in pay. This was crucial insight and an important decision.

My thinking went something like this: Even though I earned a decent income with an excellent benefits plan, the awful truth was that for most of my career, I had seldom enjoyed my job. That was the sad fact. Looking back, those few times when I did enjoy the work occurred when I had felt highly productive, times when I either helped to develop products or deliver tangible services. And I had been doing very little of that kind of work. I finally understood that I had been engaged in the wrong sort of occupation all along.

I could hear another penny drop.

If I wanted to stay well while working for this large, bureaucratic organization, one that I viewed with my idealistic eyes as having inconsistent leadership, shifting priorities, and a general sense of inertia, I needed to switch gears completely.

I needed a fresh view. I needed the kind of work that provided me with some level of satisfaction. (What the organization got from my contribution had to come second.) My focus had to be on attracting work that was better suited to my sensibilities and temperament. Period. My efforts had to be about self-preservation. If this sounds self-serving, that's because it absolutely was. And I saw no alternative. I was clear about my intentions; I needed to be if my goal was to attract my kind of work.

After creating the participant's manual, my next project was to develop an internal website on diversity, which included designing the layout and pages, as well as writing and editing content. This was a huge project, something to really sink my teeth into.

I had rudimentary web skills from keeping my private blog, and that scant bit of knowledge gave me the confidence (some might say the chutzpah) to pitch myself as the right person for the job, winning my manager's agreement to take on the project. I was in creative heaven!

Amazingly, I wasn't scared of tackling this large project with my limited background or abilities. I knew I would ace this job. (Hadn't I spent weeks envisioning myself doing the work?) I had an unshakable faith that this opportunity was put in my path because it was right for me, right now. I just trusted Spirit.

I later learned that creativity actually plays a key role in some highly successful healing plans for depression and anxiety. According to Dr. Carrie Barron, psychiatrist and psychotherapist in New York City, "The need to create is primal." She goes on to say that, "Contentment is about maintaining an identity that integrates your creative self," and that people who spend an inordinate amount of their day engaged in cerebral activity should take care to balance that with being physically active and using their hands to make things, hopefully drawing satisfaction and a better life balance from that.

Though I came upon this information years after I had incorporated creativity into my own healing regimen, by instinct and Spirit-guidance rather than by design, it does not surprise me at all. Wouldn't it be extraordinary if this notion became common knowledge among all primary care physicians and therapists, and was prescribed to patients with mental health maladies?

Creativity has made a huge difference for me, especially in my ability to function at a high level and to sustain my wellness. Understanding the importance of creativity in my life has transformed me into a happier person. I used to feel the need to justify my spending too many hours in my creativity zone, at a minimum by making something useful. But now, I don't care about the function so much. I realize that it is the act of creating that I crave and need, of making something out of nothing with my own two hands. It's more than the satisfaction it brings; it's also about the good feeling that playing on the right side of my brain gives me.

I recall one instance in particular the year following my return to work. That morning, I was having a hard time getting my brain fired up and functioning; it felt sluggish, like the gears were not engaging properly. I missed the motivation to tackle a task that I was meant to complete that day. But rather than continue down the frustrating road to discouragement, I switched gears.

For no apparent reason other than I enjoyed the work, I began looking through pages of our website, the one I had created a few years prior and for which I was still responsible. I occupied myself with tidying up content, tweaking some pages, moving pieces from here to there and ensuring links were working properly. I spent about one hour doing this. When I finished, I detected that my mood was noticeably elevated. I no longer felt in a funk about lacking motivation, nor was I angry at my brain for its deficiency. I was in a whole different headspace. My brain felt bright, alert, energetic, motivated, and in tune. I felt charged and drastically changed! The gears were clicking in.

I picked up the task that I had abandoned earlier and I ran through it like I was on fire. I could feel a palpable difference in my brain. In my mood, yes, and in my attitude and thoughts for sure, but I also could feel the difference right in my brain! There was sharpness in the way my brain was processing information; it was alert and happy. It felt bright like sparkling eyes inside the brain, in contrast to an hour before when my brain felt dull. Because it *was* dull.

That's when I understood in a tangible way the positive effect that creativity can have on the brain—certainly that it has on my brain. That's when I figured out that having creative moments within each day, either at work or at home, could improve my overall capacity for work and possibly my productivity too.

This awakening was a treasure for me. My desire for creativity was no longer just a wish or a theory, not just a personal preference based on my interest; it was a real need. I had just experienced the change resulting from a little bit of stimulation to that part of the brain that is designed for creativity.

This experience taught me that I *need* creative stimulation. If I fail to engage in some form of creativity for a few days, I feel bogged down in my thinking, and my brain starts to feel dull and slow. I also begin to feel anxiety related to my lackluster performance. I start to doubt my abilities and engage in negative self-talk: "I'm not good at this; someone else could do it twice as fast and much better than I; I'm not a good resource to the team; I shouldn't even be working anymore; I need to retire early and let someone more competent take my job," and so on. My inside voice spirals down, reaching deeper into darkness, leading me to despair. That's how quickly the mood can turn.

On the other hand, when I introduce a creative task during a period of murky thinking, the negative thinking disappears. In an instant, the mental sloth is transformed into bright thinking. I not only perform better but I feel better about myself, about my aptitudes, and about my contribution. The contrast is stunning.

"Awareness is conscious connection with universal intelligence."
—Eckhart Tolle

Personally, I believe that having creativity as part of my workload should be a requirement of my workplace accommodation rather than just a nice thing to have. But one needs to choose one's battles.

Feeling fortunate to have creative work as part of my job—as editor for our branch website—I gladly design pages and work with subject matter experts to develop their content. It is not as creative as designing costumes for a theater group or creating one-of-a-kind hats (both part of my creative history), but it's enough.

Visualization as a Tool

Visualization was an important facet in my recovery. If I could clearly picture myself doing a certain thing or being in a specific place, I felt that I probably could make that happen in reality.

I signed up for Sonia Choquette's course. In a series of structured video lessons, she teaches the steps for making a passionate desire come true. I was working through the steps for my dream of establishing a home-based business making draperies and window treatments, as an alternative to returning to my unsatisfying and stress-filled job.

The course's premise is that, energetically, we attract what we put out there. The steps guide you through ridding your mind of negative beliefs and thoughts, especially those about yourself and what you are capable of, and replacing them with positive ones and, most important, with a clear picture of your heart's desire as if it were already a reality. The more your energy vibrates at a high level, like when you are happy and grateful, the better you will attract what you desire and express.

Working with a goal that your heart passionately desires is central for two reasons. One, passion vibrates at the highest level. Two, passion also might indicate where the Divine is present. I've come to believe, as Sonia suggests, that where there is passion, there is God. This concept opened up possibilities for me. Imagine the delight that serving a divine purpose takes on, especially when your passionate interests get to tag along and contribute to the good? So, *which comes first?* I wonder. Does God's hand create the passion or does the passion attract God's presence? I don't have an answer to that, and I prefer to keep it a mystery. Either way works for me.

I wrote a jingle for my dream business and sang it repeatedly throughout the day, as instructed (because Spirit loves rhymes and music—energetically, they appear to be one of the easier-to-receive vibrational communication methods).

It was a daily challenge to raise my vibration, given that I was in the midst of generalized anxiety underlined with depression. But I pushed forth and diligently did my lessons. I was determined to get myself out of the muck of depression and I would try anything that might help. I thought of it as a game.

I had a large worktable built in our house for laying out and cutting fabric. I bought proper sewing tables for the three machines I would be using (a serger for finishing edges quickly, an industrial hemmer for a professional hem, and a multipurpose, heavy-duty sewing machine for the rest). I visualized my drapery workroom down to the minutest detail.

I visualized my clients and how pleased they were with the draperies and valances I'd made for them. I even visualized having to make adjustments to a window treatment to better suit a customer's preference. I imagined an income at a lower level than what my job paid, and I was satisfied with that because I could see that being a happier person was a worthwhile exchange. I saw all of this in my imagination and I spent hours picturing it.

I chose to return to my job in the end, concluding that running a small business—even one that meant handling the beautiful fabrics I loved—would carry great stress, probably more than what I experienced in my job and certainly more than I could sustain in the long term. I was still in a fragile emotional state. Even though the *idea* of the work appealed to me, it was the wrong time to venture out on my own. I remain thankful that I realized this fairly soon, which gave me the time to refocus my attention on seeking the right kind of work for me.

Nevertheless, learning the process of visualization and

practicing the rest of what I learned from the "Creating Your Heart's Desire" course were hugely important skills to have acquired.

I began to wonder what would happen if I applied these new skills to preparing my mind not only for returning to work, but also for correcting my work environment. I wanted to see if the same techniques could work with a real, life-making-or-breaking situation. What did I have to lose? I still had time on my side for practicing.

I immediately set myself to the task. I imagined a neutral attitude toward my work, and especially toward the organization where I had spent the last nineteen years. Both my family doctor and my CBT therapist had advised that since I, alone, could not change such a large organization, I would be wise to change myself—more exactly, to change my attitude toward it.

I started by recalling previous jobs that I had held and zeroed in on what specific tasks, if any, I had enjoyed. I came up with several and grouped them by type of work. (For instance, rewriting and editing colleagues' work at my manager's request; writing content and designing layouts for an internal website; converting memos and documents written in bureaucratic jargon to plain language; producing fact sheets; reviewing translated documents and websites; and organizing and hosting conferences for bilingual employees.) I asked myself, what did the tasks have in common and how were they linked?

I then switched gears, visualizing tasks that immediately raised my anxiety level and listed those; analyzing what precisely triggered my stress response would come later.

I now had two buckets—the tasks I felt good about doing (and wanted to attract) and those that raised my stress level (and needed to avoid). Since the idea was to focus only on what I wanted to attract, I simply ignored the tasks that caused anxiety or threatened my equilibrium.

It was important for me to get a fresh start at work after my one-year leave, and that meant having a different cubicle, in a different part of the organization, with a different focus. I knew I would return to the workplace under a work-hardening program—having been through the process twice already—and this included finding a good fit, not only specific to the work I would be assigned but also in getting a fresh start in all respects. Going back to my old cubicle probably would engender some of the old feelings of anxiety and overload, and I wanted to avoid that. I wanted to have a fighting chance, and my manager was supportive of my desire for change.

I began visualizing myself in a new workspace, one that was shiny clean and surrounded by windows with a view of the Otonabee River running through a verdant, tree-lined valley below. Why not imagine something beautiful while I was at it? It was a quiet space where I felt supported by my colleagues, whose cubicles surrounded mine. I imagined myself doing creative work using lots of color. (I love playing with colors in my fiber-related hobbies, whether it is making garments, blending colors for spinning wool, combining fabrics in a quilt, or painting my own designs on the fabric itself—I love it all.) I saw myself being calm and content, feeling productive and satisfied at the end of a workday. I visualized what I wore to work on a given day and listened to the murmur of voices in the hallway. I felt the cool surface of my desk as I placed my hands down. I used all of my senses to give my vision a true sense of reality. I imagined how I felt, what I thought about, what I saw and heard while sitting there, how the papers in my hands felt, how perfectly my chair supported my back. I also visualized myself from the outside, what I looked like, how my hair was cut, and what surrounded me besides my desk.

I stayed in that make-believe place for a good twenty minutes the first time I visited. I returned daily and added details primarily about the work I was doing at my computer, what new things were on my desk, having a colleague come to my cubicle to ask a question, and returning to my desk from my lunch break with a glad heart, ready to begin where I had left off in my work. I imagined working on a website, creating attractive pages and filling them with text, images, and links.

The visualizing exercise helped me to believe that such a workplace was possible for me because it was believable in my imagination and felt tangible. And it helped me to stay away from fretting and recalling the bad experiences that had triggered my illness to flare up this third time.

Interestingly, today my job very much resembles what I described above, except for the river view, which I gave up for my colleague Heather, who needed it more than I.

Visualization and Creation
You cannot create what you cannot imagine.

Indeed, being able to imagine the desired outcome or situation in your mind's eye, and the associated feelings within your body, is the first step in making that thing happen for yourself. Athletes use this technique, as do stage actors for developing their characters; students use it to prepare for oral and written exams, and professionals rely on it before interviewing for their dream job. When there is something important that you want, which perhaps is causing you to feel the jitters, visualization is a great technique for gearing yourself up to succeed.

I spent hours over many weeks visualizing different aspects of my future workplace and environment. When I returned to my fictional workplace, I imagined how it would be if I had a job that made me feel useful and productive. I pictured myself there and I asked: How would it be if I were able to use my natural creative abilities as part of my work? How would it be to sit in a workspace that felt good, that had a beautiful view, a place where I could do my best work, and where my full potential was realized?

It was fun to visualize such a space, just as when a child plays an imagination game. The practice taught me that it *was* possible for me to do work that was a better fit, that this kind of work *did* exist. Oh, the joy of having a job in which I could do more than survive, but where I could thrive and perhaps even contribute to the larger good. A job that made me feel good about myself.

Through similar visualization sessions, I prepared my every nerve ending—my sensing antennae—to recognize opportunities that might fit the bill for me, sometimes before the possibilities even presented themselves. And when they came my way, I recognized them as the manifestation of all my prep work. It was like I could sniff out the opportunities meant for me.

It was through this process that I landed the task of designing that sixty-page manual and how I got the job of developing an internal website, which eventually led to my role as web editor for the entire branch site.

I have been doing website work for nearly six years now, and I couldn't be happier. The work allows me to connect with my colleagues in a creative and productive way. It also enables me to provide a needed service for rendering clear communication, and most important, it requires that I exercise my creative brain.

I find the work satisfying and fulfilling. I am a contented and helpful employee, able to let my personality shine. I am certainly a different person at work now, as well as at home, because I have found the right type of work that suits my skills and temperament.

The process that I used in landing this work has affirmed my personal sense of knowing and doing, a secondary but powerful and gratifying outcome. And it has done wonders for building my self-confidence.

I am convinced that none of this could have happened had I not visualized it first. I wouldn't have known what projects to go after without having first tested my full-body response through my imagination. If this isn't magic, then I'm not sure what is.

I also use visualization to check in with myself in advance of potentially uncomfortable or challenging situations and to practice my calming responses to circumstances that make me nervous or anxious. In this way, I am usually able to diffuse my emotional discomfort in advance. Visualization can work to provide a counterbalance to what are often ready-made, preconceived ideas and fears that we have constructed for ourselves over many years. It's a way to give goodness a chance to affect a perceived negative situation or outcome. And it's a way to circumvent ego in her desire to keep the *status quo*.

CREATING YOUR HEART'S DESIRE

I credit Sonia Choquette with helping me begin to ask, and answer, the question: What do I really want out of life? I resonated with her wisdom that our sixth sense should be our first, and that our imaginations are like a muscle that benefits from exercise. The more we use our imaginations, the better we can be at imagining possibilities for ourselves, and the greater our creativity becomes overall.

It's about exercising the right side of the brain as much as the left, if not more. Even Einstein knew this. I read that whenever Einstein felt stuck on a mathematical problem, he would leave his worktable and go play the violin for a while. This musical interlude would help him become unstuck, and when he returned to work he was usually able to solve the problem with ease. According to this genius scientist, "Imagination is everything. It is the preview of life's coming attractions."

Sonia Choquette's course taught me how to explore the imagination. It taught me that I could create what I really wanted, and not to limit myself to what I thought I could get. I imagined the possibilities and thoroughly enjoyed putting the nine principles into daily practice.

It taught me to feel comfortable with the idea of being successful, and to avoid giving mental real estate to my fears. Of course I had fears, lots of them, but I learned how to allow them to just sit there and not allow them to intimidate me. I learned that my fears could not stop me unless I gave them permission to do so.

I learned that the intellect does not actually create stuff; it's the heart that does. I learned that the human spirit is a divine gift and the intellect its servant. I learned how to work within that paradigm and to recognize when it's time to bring in the intellect and let it do what it does best—think, plan, follow through, keep me accountable.

This course confirmed what I used to know: that often, what we carry in the intellect is not even ours but could be inadvertently acquired ideas. These ideas are frequently old and no longer useful. Though they might have served a purpose at some point in our lives, they might no longer serve us well, and it could be time for these old thoughts to leave us now.

The course taught me how to shape intention, beginning with a vague notion and progressing toward the most definitive creative intent. I learned that having a clear focus charged with emotion is like holding a magic wand, and that having a super-precise focus could pull in my desire as if I were turning on a powerful magnet.

I learned to discipline my thoughts in a manner that influenced my subconscious mind and helped it to come on board, that the subconscious takes pleasure in hearing rhymes, repetition, and songs. I learned to have fun with creativity, to make a game of it in an effort to engage my subconscious. I learned that creativity could be like a dance, and the more I sang my little tunes, the more my subconscious mind would play along and create *with* me.

I spoke Sonia's mantra to myself, out loud, as often as I remembered, especially when driving by myself. I wrote the words on the inside cover of my journal so they were always available as a reminder:

> I am a creator. Yes, I am.
> I am greatness. Yes, I am.
> I am successful. Yes, I am.
> I manifest better than I thought I would. Yes, I do.
> I am talented. Yes, I am.
> I am having fun at manifesting. I sure am!

I attract things easily. Yes, I do.

My subconscious mind is busy making my dream happen. Yes, it is!

I needed what Sonia calls "believing eyes," because as she explained, "Every single person who has ever succeeded in anything had believing eyes"—someone who believed in them and their idea. I wanted my own believing eyes so I recruited some (my sisters Anne and Lorraine, cousin Elvira, and especially my friends Sue and Heather).

I learned that in order to make imagination pliable and flexible, I had to work with it, to condition it to become more active. Imagination was like a cup made ready to hold all that I put into it. I used my imagination a lot, the way I remember doing as a kindergarten kid. I invited some of my believing eyes to play imagination games with me—and they loved doing it!

I learned and practiced what was required under each of the nine principles. Although I ended up dissolving my original heart's desire—to open a custom drapery business—the lessons were invaluable in making another dream come true: to land a job that required my natural creative talent and where I felt productive.

THE NINE PRINCIPLES

1. Bring your dream into focus
2. Gain the support of your subconscious mind
3. Imagine your heart's desire
4. Eliminate your obstacles
5. Be open to intuitive guidance
6. Choose to support your dream with love
7. Surrender control

8. Claim your dream

9. Stay true to your dream

I plastered sticky notes all over the house to remind me and my brain of my new thinking. The notes, especially when said out loud, also helped convince my subconscious of the new thoughts.

I surrounded myself with positive messages and images that supported my heart's desire. (Remember, I had a lot of negative thinking to neutralize, so there was no such thing as too much positive input.) On the inside cover of my journal, I pasted a lovely image of a woman celebrating the joy of life, arms extended and displaying a glowing smile, face turned upward toward the grand universe. This lovely, modern-day woman lived in connection to Spirit. She represented the person I wanted to be, the one I wanted to transform into: joyful, self-confident, carefree, beautiful, spirit-centered, fully alive and in her element, a happy, kind, loving, and generous soul—and a redhead to boot (like I used to be before turning gray). I still love this image, and it continues to bring a smile to my face.

You need to know that when I first glued her in my book in 2009, I was far from feeling remotely like her. Still, she was my inspiration and she was good for me. She encapsulated the joy I yearned for. Today, I can honestly say I do feel like her most days. And that is a measurable distance from where I once was.

I had fun creating my personal creed and a few silly jingles.

• • • EXERCISES • • •

The Job of My Desire

The exercise called "Naming my Desire" is part of the "Creating Your Heart's Desire" course. It is part of visualizing the outcome you want and being clear about why you want it. I pulled the list below from a journal entry, dated August 26, 2010.

This is what I desire regarding my job:

- I want work that keeps my interest—because it's healthy to feel engaged.
- I want a job that I enjoy and that I feel good about—because that feeds my self-esteem and confidence.
- I want a supportive work environment—because then I can be myself and contribute my energy and shining light.
- I want to do work I am good at—because I want to contribute something of value.
- I want to feel financially secure—to calm Robert's worry.
- I want a job that is a good fit and that uses my skills and talents—because then I can do good work and become healthier mentally.
- I want all of this so that my marriage can benefit from the stability, and R. & I can work together at finding our peace and building a strong marriage.

My Credo

Succeed I will, there is no doubt!
Having a partner is what it's about.
Connecting with Spirit, the key to my dream.
My partner is Admiral, we are a team!

I later added...

In silence we meet, he teaches me well,
That growing my talent is service, how swell!

Jingles

1. To the tune of the children's rhyme "Ring around the Rosie"
MaBelle, MaBelle

My curtains are swell.
Do tell, ring the bell.
All will come to order some!

2. To the tune of a children's skipping rope rhyme
Making money
Is sweet as honey.
But don't get crazy
Like Ding Dong Daisy!*

A Few Intentions and Beliefs

- I attract all that I need through divine grace.
- I am a successful co-creator of my own reality.
- I am ready for a gift; I am open for a gift; I am eager to receive a gift; I expect a gift; and I enjoy my gift from the universe.
- I feel fulfilled and peaceful in every way.
- I have a beautiful, creative mind.
- I believe there is enough prosperity in this world to include me.
- I believe I will receive good news today.
- I believe in my happiness.
- I believe I can; I believe in my progress.

I wrote these personal beliefs in my journal:
- Success is… being fulfilled in my work, home, and spiritual life.
- Money is… for a secure financial future that includes some travel and flexibility to be free and do stuff.

---

* This refers to our silly dog named Daisy, who is no longer with us.

• Health is… both mental and in body, requiring balance with spirit.

• Happiness is… a balance with joy, healthy relationships with a life partner, family, and good friends.

• Peace is… being one with Spirit, sitting in God's lap.

• Creativity is… connecting with my inner light and tuning in to Spirit's guidance.

IMAGINATION PLAY

I recall an evening when some friends were at my house for one of our knitting-with-tea gatherings. With sneaked permission, I hijacked the meeting and took them to "Imagination Land." (I even gave them each a handmade "train ticket" to add some authenticity!) I led them through a visualization exercise by imagining the perfect house for sale at the right price for Sue. (Sue had been in the market for a while and had been unsuccessful in finding the right house.)

I led them to a pretty, tree-lined street where a real estate agent waited to take us through a perfect-looking house. We made our way along the concrete walk, climbed the steps to the front porch, and opened a wooden screen door. Once inside, we took our shoes off and proceeded through the foyer. I noted an oval-shaped, amber-colored window that let a golden ray of light shine onto the combined living-dining room's hardwood floor. We followed the agent to the neat, mint-green kitchen at the back of the house. I knew this room suited Sue's taste perfectly, like the 1950s kitchen she remembered from her childhood home. There were large sash windows on three sides of the room, offering an unobstructed view of the treed yard out back, with flowerbeds and an herb garden along the deck.

The sweet scent of cinnamon wafted through (good smells must waft) to clinch the experience.

But that's not all. This kitchen was big enough to accommodate an old-style rocking chair that Sue loved for petting her cats, Bailey and O'Malley. There were a dozen freshly filled jars of preserves on the counter by the double sink, looking very much like strawberry-rhubarb. The floors gleamed under the braided area rugs. The house was neat as a pin and a pleasure to view. We all felt this was the perfect house for Sue.

I supplied more detail as we entered every room and described the many things Sue was hoping for in her next home.

I gently brought us back to reality, tempting as it was to stay in Imagination Land. But it would soon be time to call it a night and I wanted to get their feedback on the experience. They loved it and thought it was fun. It reminded me of story time in kindergarten when the teacher told a story while the children lay down on their towels or blankets, a comforting remembrance.

I am grateful to be a searching soul with a trusting temperament and a perceptive nature. Given that, seeking to know and understand God has been a natural path for me, and a fulfilling, ongoing journey.

Expressing gratitude each day does more than remind me to appreciate all that I have, especially the good people in my life. It also serves to raise my energetic vibration and by doing so, to attract more of the same. If nothing else, as I get my day into gear each morning, I spend some quiet time in gratitude. If I don't have time for a full meditation, I spend at least three minutes being thankful. This little timeout sets the tone for my day and escorts me out the door with a song in my heart.

I am grateful to have discovered one of God's best-kept secrets—that he is the best therapist and personal coach available! I've spent more than a few dollars on psychotherapy over the years. That has led me to better understand some old wounds and has taught me techniques for letting go of the pain. It helped me see things through fresh eyes. It taught me to recognize nonproductive patterns in my life and to view difficult circumstances with a new lens. Sometimes, I just needed a compassionate, neutral person to talk to, someone who understood my history and baggage and who would not judge me. I paid a lot for that privilege.

Today, I have access to the best-ever healer for the mind and soul, and the service is offered free of charge. The only prerequisites are a deep faith in that higher power and the ability to relinquish control.

> "By thanking God, the universe, or our own grasp of the 'Higher Power,' we remain doubly sensitive to the positive aspects of our journey while reassuring our inner self that our spiritual path is being confirmed."
>
> —Tom Harpur

The deepest and most pervasive healing I have ever experienced came from God. Best of all—next to being free—is his 24/7 availability anywhere in the world. No appointment is necessary, just some time spent each day in what author Matthew Kelly calls the "classroom of silence." Committing to growing a personal understanding and relationship with God is necessary, for before he will work with you, he needs to trust you, and you, him.

I thank him, my savior of spirit and soul, for guiding me to a healthy workplace, where I earn a respectable wage and enjoy responsible work that is well-suited to my skills, abilities, and temperament. I am grateful for my fantastic colleagues and for having the time to start my days in morning meditation, a true luxury in our busy world.

In reviewing my 2010 journals for writing this book, I recalled an incident that I hadn't thought about since, and one that I cherish. I've mentioned that I've always felt a deep pain in my heart whenever I got too close to loving someone completely. My heart felt real pain, along with a fear and vulnerability of an infant child. I would break down in tears and not be able to explain exactly why, other than feeling too raw. It was frustrating because my mind wanted the intimacy, but my heart held back. I couldn't help it—it just happened that way. It made me sad because I really wanted to love someone with my entire being, but no amount of therapy had managed to clear that hurt away. Thankfully, my husband understood and accepted this as part of the authentic person he married.

On this particular afternoon, I was putting final touches on my sewing workroom, moving storage shelves and hanging pictures that depicted joy, which I hoped would inspire creativity and productiveness in this sacred space. I held a photo of my son, Marcel, at age four with his beautiful face in full, exuberant smile, set in a *papier-mâché* frame in the shape of a sun. I hung that picture beside one of his sister at age five, looking so happy and proud to be standing with her arm around her mommy's neck, and a third picture of both Caroline and Marcel at Marcel's high school graduation. Well, I felt so proud of those kids that the tears started streaming down my cheeks.

That's when I felt my soul open up to the extreme love I feel for my children, no matter how old they get. For ten minutes, I bawled my eyes out, sobbing for no apparent reason. (There were no issues between us that might have caused me grief.) I knew something big was taking place, because as I experienced the deep love for my son and daughter, I simultaneously felt a close connection to Spirit. I could sense deep within me that something important was taking place.

I later understood that it was the healing of my heart that was taking place. And I promise you, I haven't feared or held back from deep love since that day: March 30, 2010.

From that moment, I was able to start loving my husband in a complete and confident way, not just part-way but all the way, holding nothing back. And because I was able to give him all of me, which I like to think is what he needed, he was able to openly and completely reciprocate. Our love for each other became freer, able to take a deeper, more fulfilling turn.

> "The happiness of your life depends upon the quality of your thoughts."
>
> —Marcus Aurelius

Remember the God-wink incident I mentioned regarding the online radio call-in show with Sonia Choquette? When Spirit facilitated the answer to my question that day, telling me that my job in my marriage was simply to love my husband, I first needed my heart to be healed in order to do that job properly.

That's how I have found God to work in my life. It all seems so obvious when looking back, but things are not nearly so clear while the magic is taking place. And that's where the act of surrendering to trust comes into play. I don't think God works nearly as well without that.

Sometimes, doesn't it seem that he takes his sweet time doling out the magic? Yet, other times, things happen so fast it's breathtaking. I have even needed to call a halt to the manifestations so I could catch my breath.

CO-CREATION

During my "sabbatical," I practiced using the skills I was learning and turned my focus on co-creating a new, healthful, and creative life for myself. I practiced vibrating at a high frequency all the time. I found that as I attracted specific good things into my life, the momentum of attraction built and the manifestations increased in number and speed. My practice was fully integrated into every minute of my day-to-day world. (Have I mentioned that I am a determined person?) I felt fully engaged in creating a positive, exciting, divine lifestyle, giving of my talent, and keeping my soul happy. I felt like I was splashing this amazing manifestation all over the place! Like finding thirteen-dollar rollerblades in the local thrift store the day after saying that I wanted skates to explore our new neighborhood; or knowing that I would run into my cousin and her husband, who live ninety minutes away, just before it happened; or the time I took a different, roundabout route to the grocery store for no apparent reason, only to come upon a garage sale with the perfect table for my new plants. My life was filled with serendipitous occurrences. It was fun just watching it all unfold.

More recently, at about the same time I reengaged my passion for writing this book, having let it go untouched for almost a year, I consciously reconnected with my co-creative skills. Since that moment of choice, the manifestations began occurring at a crazy rate, again. The impetus for picking up my writing again was something that Elizabeth Gilbert said in an interview about her book *Big Magic*—that inspiration won't necessarily hang around forever waiting for you to turn an idea into action; that inspiration could well decide to look for another, more willing partner, one who was ready to move on the idea right now (because inspiration is excited and impatient).

It was New Year's Day 2016, following a call from my sister Anne about an interview with Gilbert on CBC radio, which I immediately downloaded. Well, that lit the fire under me in a big way; I did *not* want someone else to write this story, nor to lose the inspiration to tell it my way.

"As I believe, so I receive."

—Sonia Choquette

Here is how the incredible serendipitous connections surrounding my book played out: Sometime in mid-February, I decided to be bold and contact a few authors whose work I admired, and who had figured in my healing journey. I asked if they might be interested in my book, perhaps for a review or endorsement. I wrote to four people and heard back from two: Matthew Kelly's publisher and Tom Harpur.

Kelly's publisher offered to look at a book proposal if I didn't already have a publisher lined up. (Of course I didn't!) From everything I had read, I figured it was near impossible for an unknown author like me to catch the interest of a publisher at all, let alone this early in the game. I had pretty much accepted the fact that I would be self-publishing, perhaps producing only enough copies for my friends and family and be done with it—I just wanted my story out there. I looked into buying a publishing package from a well-known and well-marketed company but decided against it when it became clear they appeared more interested in selling packages than in supporting new authors.

So yes, I was very interested in submitting a book proposal to Kelly's publisher! I felt super-grateful to have a contact, someone who wouldn't automatically slide this one-too-many query into the trash can. I worked hard over several days to pull together a proposal, having it reviewed by two writers in my family, and sending it off before this contact forgot my name! I was told to expect to wait two months before hearing back. Patience... Like I told my husband, "Regardless of the outcome of this query, the hard work I put into preparing a proposal will not have been wasted; it will just make it easier for the next query."

Meantime, I talked with Holy Spirit and explained that I really was not cut out or interested in doing all the heavy lifting required in self-publishing, the technical learning curve needed for a professional-looking digital book, the packaging, pitching, promoting, marketing, and selling the book, contacting bookstores, media for radio and TV spots, sending the book out for reviews, soliciting interview spots, guest blogging, etc. I wasn't about to retire only to pick up all this work! No, what I wanted was to immerse myself in fiber arts, spend time at the cabin, travel a bit—not push a book up a hill. I had done my share of uphill pushing while employed. No, thank you!

It was on the very day of this conversation, as I browsed the Internet for Canadian publishers accepting unsolicited manuscripts, still hoping against hope not to have to do my own book schlepping, that I came across my publisher. KiCam Projects was a brand-new American company looking for their first authors to publish. And their deadline was still three weeks away. *Imagine that,* I thought, *a deadline that had not expired!* And, get this, I saw that KiCam's mission was to bring light to people's true stories of rising from adversity, and they were looking for memoirs. I couldn't believe my eyes. I felt so sure that this was the place for me that I stopped looking.

I immediately submitted a proposal and the rest is history, as the saying goes. I am so very pleased with the relationship we built as I completed my writing. There is no doubt in my heart that the Holy Spirit had a hand in arranging this contract.

It was time to tell my manager that I was writing my story, that it would be published as a book, and that she had a part in it. I didn't want to use her real name and I thought how perfect it would be to use her second name, if I knew it, which I did not. So I chose to call her Liz because it just seemed to fit. I told my manager, and guess what her second name is? Yup, Elizabeth, or Liz. My response was, "I'm not surprised," because I had been flying on such a series of God winks those past weeks that nothing could surprise me anymore.

Having previously contacted Tom Harpur's "people" and having been told that my query was premature, and that I was welcome to come back when I had a publisher, I did exactly that. Tom Harpur not only agreed to review what I had written so far, he followed through and wrote the very kind words featured on the back cover of this book. What a gentleman, indeed! And what a kind God-gesture, for which I am so grateful and super-charged!

That's when I asked for all the goodness to hold the show for a while; I needed respite from the speed of love! I needed to catch my breath and spend time writing so I could finish a first draft. I would begin working with a developmental editor soon and I wasn't ready.

I can hardly express my gratitude...
• For the determined part of me that pushes to where I need to be
  • For my Spirit teacher of spiritual growth
  • For my fire and earth energy—I love them both
  • For each of my siblings, who have love in their hearts
  • For having such a supportive and loving husband

- For being able to find peace in times of uncertainty
- And especially, I am forever grateful to know God and be growing in our relationship

••• EXERCISES •••

1. List ten people in your life whom you truly appreciate, and write what it is, specifically, that you appreciate about them, and why.

2. When tackling a problem, practice focusing on the vibration of the solution, not that of the problem.

3. Gratitude also will raise your vibration and attract more of the same. Keep a daily gratitude journal, and note even the small things for which you are grateful in your day and in your life. Don't worry if it feels awkward at first. Once you notice your days becoming more positive, it will feel more natural.

I've always liked a certain amount of structure in my life, not too much but some; it offers a level of security I suppose. In any case, I seem to need it. But the type of structure I was looking for during my year of healing in 2010 would need to allow plenty of flexibility to accommodate the unforeseen and be geared to capturing opportunities for growth—especially the Spirit-led ones.

Imagine my delight when I happened onto Cheryl Thiele's *The Sacred Journey: Daily Journal for Your Soul* at our local bookstore—and at half price to boot! I had never come across this book before even though it was in its fifteenth edition at the time. The book had everything I was hoping for in a planner/journal and so much more. It offered a daily structure and guided me though a journaling process. It helped me to go deeper into certain spiritual areas, make note of insights, and turn challenges into opportunities, and it provided thought-provoking questions for monthly introspection and review.

The book also offered guidance in some areas of interest:

• On creativity: "When we follow through with our creative ideas, we open to the powers of serendipity and synchronicity."

• On intuition: "The more you respond to your intuition, the stronger it becomes. Intuition is the juice for 'growing with the flow.'"

• On symbolism, and using oracle cards as a way to tap into the higher self's wisdom, for obtaining guidance and clarity from a trusted source.

• On establishing goals and using affirmations to help set the tone for my life.

During this period, all the days were mine to arrange as I wished. Other than shopping for groceries and cooking for Robert and me, my job was to get well. I scheduled my days around medical appointments, which I limited to one per day when possible, because anything more would drain me to the point of exhaustion.

I put into practice what I was learning from my cognitive behavior therapist, whom I saw monthly. Although CBT was not new to me, having learned about this therapeutic technique in 2003 during an eight-week group program for those with depression, working with Dr. Wilkins was my first attempt at applying the technique on active symptoms. (By the time my name made it to the top of the wait list in 2003, my depression had already lifted.)

> "We were born to make manifest the glory of God that is within us. And as we let our own light shine, we unconsciously give other people permission to do the same. As we are liberated from our own fear, our presence automatically liberates others."
> —Marianne Williamson

I rigorously practiced positive thinking through any and all interactions with the outside world as well as privately with my own thoughts as I went about my daily routine. I spent a great amount of time inside my head, observing mostly negative thoughts and thought patterns, searching for and identifying their source, adjusting and correcting thoughts where appropriate, and replacing old thinking with new, more truthful and accurate thoughts. I learned to use the simplest of techniques like wearing an elastic band loosely around my wrist and snapping it at the onset of a negative thought to arrest it—the sound and sensation on the wrist reinforcing the message to the brain that this thought was not acceptable—and replacing wrong thinking with more realistic and truthful thoughts. It was grueling work and I felt proud of my progress, especially of my perseverance. I was nothing if not determined to lick this.

I kept a record of my progress, of what I was learning, of the insights I picked up from doctors and from reading; I wrote about my thinking, my feelings, and my frustrations; I jotted down my goals and a focus for each day, week, and month. Journaling helped me release what I referred to as emotional junk—better to have that stuff on paper and away from spinning around and cluttering my already busy and jumbled mind.

What I wrote made the new thinking seem more real to me through observing the words on paper. And creating a record of my thinking was important, because when I recorded my positive outlook for a given day, by the following day, if my mood had turned dark, I might not believe that the positive outlook had actually happened. Reading a journal entry served as proof that I was capable of a positive outlook and that it had been real and true only yesterday. My journal helped me to recognize and accept my capacity to travel through a range of moods, rather than limit my beliefs exclusively to the dark days.

I had a separate dream journal for making notes of my nighttime dreams, and I tried to learn from them. Believing that dreams are a preferred platform for the spiritual world when attempting to communicate with earthly beings, I watched for signs and symbols that could shed light on my situation. I used a trusted dream dictionary to better understand the role of key players and possible meanings for symbols. I wanted to learn all I could from both my subconscious as well as my conscious mind.

> "It is only through the heart that one can see rightly; what is essential is invisible to the eye."
> —Antoine de Saint-Exupéry

I tuned in to all of my senses including my sixth sense, to glean every possible piece of information.

I was determined that this would be my last pass through this particular life experience. I spent the year learning how to manage my thoughts. It was hard, continuous work. And I was getting good at it. I knew what had to be done to keep my brain pointed in the right direction, and I thought I was achieving it. That is, until my husband suggested otherwise. More on that later.

MY SPIRIT'S BACK-TO-HEALTH JOURNEY

I set an intention for my private blog/journal: to create a positive space where intentions are launched and manifestations are joyfully recorded, a place where Divine Spirit is present, lovingly providing guidance. It's a happening place!

I determined to journal on the positive developments not only in my work life but in all aspects of my life—spirituality, home, mental health, creativity, family, friendships, and community— with the goal of maintaining B-A-L-A-N-C-E, that oh-so-important and sometimes elusive state.

SAMPLE BLOG ENTRIES

In this space, I will post inspirational words and list positive and constructive thoughts. I will document my daily accomplishments however small they may seem (because even little things can have a huge impact on my brain and what it believes. Remember, what I think about expands). I will shape my steps one day at a time and focus on my progress. My steps are small and constant.

I invite my higher self and Spirit to work with me and guide me as I enter this part of my journey; I invite you to speak to me though my writing here, help me find the perfect resources as I need them, and keep me on track. I ask for your help and guidance.

March 30, 2010 | Awakening
I am immeasurably thankful to have experienced this awakening as a result of my illness. I knew I wanted to retrain my mind and see the world through different eyes. But I didn't know it would lead to such joy and fulfillment. Thankfully, I knew to trust and to follow guidance in whatever direction. I knew I needed to sever my need for validation by others because that was keeping me back, keeping me from growing, keeping me from my beautiful potential.

I would like to mark through ceremony my engagement on this new, Spirit-led path. I feel it's a marriage, where my expansion is the center of my existence here on earth. The people in my life may come and go, but my partnership with Spirit (whom I sometimes call Admiral) is a life-long bond!

It feels like an awakening, a rebirth, and a perfect balance of spirit, body, mind, good work, friendships, family, and service.

August 20, 2010 | *I Control My Thoughts*
Because I know that I control my thoughts, why wouldn't I use the same techniques that I have been learning and practicing these past eight months for directing my thoughts in managing my anxiety? I think that's a terrific idea!

I created the MaBelle blog (my drapery business' private blog) precisely to help keep me focused on my goal by paying more attention to the positive steps I was making and less on negative and nervous thoughts that tend to find their way through. Making changes to the way a person thinks is a process with some steps forward and some steps back. Because my tendency is to pay more attention to negative thinking (I understand this is common among us humans), giving more brain time to the backward steps than to the steps forward, I wanted to reverse that. I started to consciously change my thoughts in January, and the MaBelle blog supported this new mindful strategy.

Because what we think about expands, the more I think of positive and energetic thoughts and the more energy I put into that, the more I am able to think more positive thoughts. The reverse is horribly true as well, but I won't go there in this blog because that idea gets way too much air time already. This blog is a space to capture my much-deserving positive self-talk and self-love. And who else but me can give me self-love? If I enjoy showing love and appreciation to others, then I should be able to do at least as much for myself. I MUST do this for me.

September 23, 2010

Frustration at the slowness of the return-to-work process. My doctor/therapist's advice was the Serenity Prayer (God grant me the serenity to accept the things I cannot change, the courage to change the things I can, and wisdom to know the difference).

There is a level of acceptance that needs to happen for me to return to work. I need to decide how my job is going to be meaningful and productive. When things don't go at the pace I would like, I need to wait until the ball gets returned and to let go of my need to have it go at my pace. I'm learning that letting go is not about burying my feelings about work, or avoiding the pain or difficult experience, nor is it about giving in or giving up; it simply means moving on. I need to change in my head if I am going to go back to that work environment. I've been stuck in the same place of frustration for far too long. It means taking hold of that painful energy and transforming it into something else, something that serves me rather than destroys me.

September 25, 2010

I will write more about this transformation as I learn more through doing it. I must not allow the work situation to extinguish my inner light. How to do it, how to do it? I ask for inspiration and help in learning to do this. My Spirit teacher, I ask for your guidance in this area.

October 12, 2010 | *Making Fun*

Meantime, I taught myself how to make awesome apple pies! I'm on my third—one is in the freezer for Christmas—and there are enough down-home apples left for two more pies. How utterly satisfying this baking thing has been. And my Robbie is very pleased too!

October 4, 2010 | The Wonder of Drugs
I think my mood is stabilizing on neutral-to-good since taking Cymbalta; I'm still working with the side effects though. If my mood can stay out of the doldrums, then I want to continue with it for many years. Wouldn't it be wonderful to feel confident in my mood for more than one day at a time, to make plans and be reasonably sure that I will be mentally and emotionally able to follow through? And not feel like a prisoner to my mood swings, to be free of the shackles? I would surely like that.

November 4, 2010
I've been taking Cymbalta for six weeks now and my thinking is sharper, my mood is much improved and feels stabilized. If this is sustained, I will feel like a new person. (I feel like a new person now, but I'm being cautious in my optimism because I haven't taken the ultimate test yet, and that is when I return to work.) It's nuts that I have been trying to get back to work for two and a half months, and they are just dragging their heels! They are not even returning my calls.

It looks like the union may get involved in my return-to-work case if I don't hear anything by Monday. I am applying my doctor's lesson from the Serenity Prayer, to do what I can and then let it go. It doesn't mean I'm not pursuing my options and pushing for resolution, but the process is not playing with my emotions. And that feels very different. I know the medication is playing a key role in this.

November 27, 2010 | A Roaring Success
My first week back to work was a roaring success! And best of all, I am loving the work! I'm editing Employee Engagement content for the employee website and am about to begin a

project to create an orientation guide for the ministry's Diversity Mentoring program. Publisher is such fun software to use that it's like playing!

My forty-minute walk to work is an added bonus and I enjoy that tremendously.

How wonderful life is when all the pieces light up like the stars in the sky—especially with a job that is aligned with my talents and abilities, and I can be my best self in all areas of my life. That's when I experience the joy of balance. Ah... that is heaven on earth to me. When spirit, body, soul, and heart, creativity, health, joy, and giving are all singing together, what a lovely place it is to be. I know that is how life was designed to be. Hallelujah!

I will increase my hours next week and eventually build to full days, and maybe even increase from three to four days per week at some point. But, I must be careful not to go too fast, because I do get pretty keen and excited. I must remember to be gentle with myself and find the middle ground, nice 'n' easy.

I look forward to work on Monday. (Who said that?!)

December 8, 2010
I'm playing with penguins in my Joy Room today, making a red Christmas tree skirt out of bright-colored felt.

January 7, 2011
Work has been going fantastic! And gangbusters too! We are very busy, especially in the Diversity program. As the writer responsible for the new website, I am part of a good team of women, including my editor from the Communications branch and the Deputy's office. They are taking quite an interest in Diversity, it seems. How nice to work on a project with a higher profile. This is another manifestation, because I had asked for

exactly that kind of work. I wanted to work only on projects the ministry is pushing, not on stuff that I need to shove upstream. Ah... what a welcome relief indeed.

And this amazing work has come about thanks to the universe responding to my signals; I've been putting energy "out there" in line with what I want and need, and I'm getting back nothing less, and even more than I could have hoped for. For example, I daydreamed of using creativity in my work, and of course that's what I've been doing since I returned to work in mid-November. I asked to use my talents with colors and design, and I am certainly doing that, and will continue in that direction by developing pages and content for the new website.

As I sign off this Friday evening, I thank Great Spirit for being always with me, for loving me, for listening to me, and especially for getting things moving for me. I am so VERY grateful. I ask that you continue to guide me and inspire me, and that you help generate perfect harmony and balance.

April 8, 2011
On Tuesday at bedtime, I asked my spirit guides to give me a clear sign of their presence so that I would know FOR SURE that they were there. Lo and behold, they woke me up in the middle of the night with a strong, cold breeze on my face that continued along my arms as I reached for the duvet at the bottom of the bed! I knew instantly that it was my guides answering my request.

How absolutely enchanting the experience was! I fell back asleep with the biggest smile on my face :) Ah, how sweet life is when you let in Divine inspiration and guidance. (P.S. The windows were all shut, this being early April and rather cool in central Ontario, and there was no fan.)

Next morning, I offered my guides a thank you gift of a pretty knitted sample using my very own hand-spun yarn. I think they appreciated the token because they know how much I enjoyed the creative process of blending colors and exploring the variety of yarns I can make by adjusting the spinning and plying, especially with the wide range of pretty colors.

June 25, 2011
Tapawingo Spiritual Retreat, Near Algonquin Park, Ontario
This was the second self-made retreat for two friends and me.

I did some personal work in advance, preparing myself with an accepting frame of mind and opening my heart to whatever presented itself. I asked Spirit to help connect the three of us soul to soul and heart to heart, and that is exactly what took place. Thank you, Spirit, for your guidance during the three days.

I marked my commitment to partnering with Divine Spirit all the days of my life with a personal pledge:

"I commit to a life-long marriage with Spirit (my Admiral); I commit to expanding my listening abilities so that I may benefit to the utmost from Spirit's wisdom and guidance; I commit to creating space in my life for Spirit to live and breathe; I commit to supporting my dear friends and family in their quests to achieving their heart's desire; I promise to try my hardest to support them in the manner they desire and deserve, rather than lead them in the ways I prefer; I pledge to be strong in my resolve, to keep my life simple by 'just doing the next right thing,' to honor differences, to love myself so that I can love others, and to give of myself to make this world a better place."

Together, we held a New Beginnings ceremony (also known as a Death and Life Arrow ceremony).

I gave the boot to:

• Judgment—replacing it with acceptance, seeking to understand, and allowing

• Control—the need to control especially at work; I pay attention only to what is within my control and allow events to unfold as they should.

I invited into my life:

• Trust—especially that my Spirit is keeping me on my path, my job being simply to hear and allow

• An Open Heart—to expand the joy, to connect with other loving and like-minded souls

• Laughter

• Listening—seeking to understand, listening between the words

January 21, 2014 | *Trouble Brewing*

Since returning to work after the Christmas break, I have been feeling worn out by work, probably due to my Team Lead's retirement in December, and feeling that I will be left holding much of the work, when I have no capacity for that. I feel that my stamina is very low. Today is January 21, twelve years to the day since my first depressive breakdown. Coincidence, perhaps, but maybe not. Anniversaries of this sort can be especially difficult.

I took the day off due to a low-grade headache, more like pressure in my head since yesterday, but mostly because my brain feels so tired from work. I think it is stress related. Am feeling the anxiety mounting and depression lurking. I feel vulnerable because I don't have my supervisor as a buffer anymore. And I don't know how to raise the alarm. I am in such a vulnerable state that I don't know how to explain this to my manager. I feel that I need a third party to explain my situation and to help determine what work I think I can do, and what work I can't.

Later the same day...

Had a two-and-a-half-hour lie-down (no sleep, simply processing the stress). I will mention my mental state to the nurse practitioner tomorrow and will suggest decreasing my work hours to three days during this period of acute stress. With increased stress, I need to increase the pressure-release valve. Well, that's how it feels anyway. My head does not feel any lighter, though, after the nap.

• • • EXERCISES • • •

The following exercises are taken from *Creative Journal Writing: The Art and Heart of Reflection* by Stephanie Dowrick (Penguin Group, 2009).

Journaling Exercise 1: Use Your Physical Senses

The memory of a situation will come into your mind with greater clarity when you tune in to your physical senses: seeing, hearing, tasting, touching, feeling, thinking, sensing.

Practice recalling a mundane circumstance through the senses as you remember them. Soon, you will find yourself paying closer attention to the senses when you are next in a situation that you might want to journal about.

- How did your body feel as you sat through the meeting?
- What was it like to be touched (physically or emotionally) at the gathering following the baby's christening?
- What was the physical environment like when you went to inquire about the new job?
- What were your feelings as you went up the stairs to the historic building?
- What kind of work environment would you name as ideal?

- What was the person's quality of voice? How did you find yourself responding to it? Was it irritating or soothing? Too soft or too loud?

Journaling Exercise 2: Recall from Memory

Describe a situation that happened several years ago. Pick something instinctively. Run it through your mind like a movie. When you begin to write, focus on what you *think* about the situation. After about five minutes, switch your focus to your feelings. Then, after another five or ten minutes, switch again to emphasize your thoughts over feelings.

Remind yourself what the place looked like, what the atmosphere was, how it smelled, if it was hot and humid or if you felt chilled. Who else was involved? What challenged, pleased, surprised, or frustrated you?

Finish by completing these sentences:

- "The sense I now have about the situation is…"
- "The memories that seem strongest for me are…"

Notice any differences between observations driven by thought and those driven by feelings. Don't reread your writing immediately. Let your thoughts "rest."

Journaling Exercise 3: Listen to Your Soul

Before you begin, light a candle, put on some relaxing music if you don't find that distracting, sit comfortably, and quiet your mind. You are honoring the sacred within.

Choose one of the topics below as your starting point for a letter (or series of letters) from your soul to you.

- What does your soul "long for"? Let your soul tell you clearly what that is and how you can achieve it.
- Which of your soul's qualities or strengths would support

you to live a life more closely aligned with the Divine, with your own spiritual aspirations?

- What does your life's purpose look like from your soul's perspective?
- What are your soul's gifts to this world?

I encourage you to draw a picture and/or add colors to your journal entry to make your writing fuller and perhaps more connected to your soul.

DEPRESSION AS AN ILLNESS

Surprisingly, the act of accepting that I had a mental illness was a freeing experience for me. It was as if the illness now had a personality of its own. I was no longer wholly responsible for my mental state because I could share the responsibility with the illness—it had its role and I had mine. It became more of a partner for understanding its evolving nature and for keeping the symptoms in check. I was not the illness, and it was not me. I was its manager, and my job was learning how to be the kind of manager it needed. I was still in charge, but I was no longer completely consumed by it. Mind you, when it was in flare-up mode, it was certainly at the forefront of my every thought and activity but only until I succeeded in managing it down again. It was about managing a cycle of aliveness and dormancy.

The trick—when it is alive—is remembering to implement the many tools I had employed before in taming it down. There is no need to feel sorry for myself, or frustrated by my lack of interest in my life or motivation. I recognize that it is just the illness attempting to take hold of my life; somewhere inside of my brain is the knowledge for how to manage it. I just need to access my self-discipline for activating the helpful keys. It is not a quick fix by any means. It takes patience and self-indulgence, but I trust myself to find the tried and tested path. I know I can climb out of the doldrums one clear step at a time and be fine again.

RISK TAKING

It was a few months into my recovery year when I got the idea to quit my government job. I would start a home-based sewing business in which I could spend my days handling beautiful fabrics—one of my all-time favorite things—and create custom window treatments for interior designers and private clients. That's what I would do!

> "Confidence comes not from always being right but from not fearing to be wrong."
> —Peter McIntyre

Truth is, the responsibility of staying in my stable, unsatisfying job had been weighing on me more than I cared to admit. And for the first time, I saw that staying with that job was a choice, not a prison—golden handcuffs perhaps, but not a death sentence. I finally saw what I had been blind to: I had a choice.

This decision was the most liberating thing I had done in twenty years and it felt awesome. Mind you, it was a giant risk, because as a freelance writer, my husband had little financial security and no health benefits. Mine was the stable income in our household, providing medical and dental benefits for the family.

I flew to North Carolina for a two-week course covering the ins and outs of establishing a drapery-making business, and how to fabricate window treatments such as valances, blinds, swags, and jabots. Who knew there was a dedicated school for this?

Spending twelve solid days learning alongside a dozen talented and like-minded women was fun and inspirational. It was an intensive and exhilarating experience from which I returned with an impressive portfolio of sample mini-drapes and window shades that I had constructed. I learned how to use industrial sewing machines and an arsenal of specialized workroom tools and equipment, from thread cones and magnetized bowls for straight pins, to blackout linings and railroaded fabric. I even learned to work with staple guns powered by compressed air—wow, do they have punch!

Once home, I immediately set up my workroom in the lower level of our bungalow—not pretty but spacious enough. The biggest commitment was having a suitable worktable built in the center of the room, large enough to accommodate the lengths of fabric I would be handling on my own. My custom-built table is five feet wide by ten feet long, is covered with a padded, pinnable surface, with storage shelves underneath for bolts of fabrics and bulky supplies. I wasted no time inscribing the name of my business on the table cover: MaBelle Interior Sewing. (The name comes from my mom calling me "*Michèle, ma belle*" which in French means "my pretty" and rhymes with my name, and is also like the lyrics of the song by The Beatles.)

Although I didn't open my business in the end, the process of considering the decision to quit my employment was important. It released my spirit from the shackles of my job (the beast responsible for causing my first breakdown and subsequent relapses!) and allowed me to explore other income possibilities. For those reasons alone, the experience was hugely beneficial.

It also taught me much about the limits and expectations I placed upon myself. My workplace caused my breakage, and it was only natural that I feared it so. But it didn't need to continue paralyzing me.

Having a table custom built was not a waste either; it continues to see plenty of use, because fabrics and all things related remain my favorite artistic medium. From creating art quilts, "painting" portraits using a broad palette of colored threads and a sewing machine, exploring surface design on fabric, and learning to weave my own textiles, my leisure activities more than justify the financial outlay.

LIVING WITHOUT FEAR

I don't feel like a loner any longer. While I continue to enjoy my own company, no question there, I also enjoy the company of good friends—a lot. There was a time in my life when I honestly did not understand the desire for friends! Isn't that a bit sad? But that's where my spirit was, constrained by an underlying, unrecognized low-grade depression. Having friends pulled me out of my comfort zone, a restrictive and limiting existence. I see that now. The truth is that my friends have enriched my life in a way I could not have conceived of before.

Sonia Choquette's course/workshop helped me define who I wanted to be and how I wanted to live in the world by focusing on some key elements:

The Thing—It is my job as co-creator to set the intention for what I want, clarify my desire, and experience the associated passion in the body, using all of my senses. Speaking out loud what I want to create, when it is accelerated by love, is the most dynamic sound (vibration) there is—and very powerful.

The How—This is where the fear comes in, which is the contraction. We want to know how it will all shake out and how much it will cost. Can I can afford it, and how will it affect my inner circle? But this is the universe's job; the Higher Power is who takes care of this part, not me.

The Why—It's the joy of expansion, the opening, the dynamic vibration, the smooth transition from past to present. It never ceases to impress and amaze me.

For every step you take, the universe matches you; it dances with your heart's desire (not with your intellect). It is our feelings that create, that activate creation; *the thing* (our desire) begins to have a life of its own with its own heartbeat.

I learned that it is important to exercise the imagination muscle, like any other muscle we want to strengthen. As children, most of us had active imaginations and we frequented them without giving it a second thought; it came naturally to us. I learned that it can be that way for us again.

If we intend to co-create a desired reality in our lives, we need to rediscover the art of imagination. We need to imagine our heart's desire as being alive and then give it a heartbeat. We need to listen for the ping as we watch that desire take shape within the imagination and in our feelings. We need to imagine it all the time throughout our day.

Our heart energy activates the vibration of joy in the body. If we "listen" for it, we can almost hear a ping, it's so perfect. It's like hearing the penny drop in our hearts or observing perfection sliding into home plate. It's something we recognize when it happens, but it's darn hard to explain it to someone who has not experienced it for himself or herself.

We can neutralize fear by asking it what it is, what it represents for me, and what it wants. Name it, and it loses its power.

With our outside voice, we name the fear, release it, and feel the vibration shift. Taking a big breath into the fear turns it into adventure. Fear is natural; everyone experiences it some-

> "Open your mind to your limitless potential."
> —Wayne Dyer

times. That doesn't mean you need to let it lead or control you. It can tag along, but it can't be in charge. You are aware of its presence, but it has lost its hold over you. It could even become a friend, one that keeps you on edge just enough to capture creative solutions.

Taking Ownership (I Am My Own Specialist)

In Western society, we have been trained to defer to doctors and other medical experts when seeking treatment; we answer their questions and wait for their instruction or prescription. While some doctors encourage patients to do their own research, we often tend to hold back on expressing our knowledge so as not to be perceived as too forceful or non-trusting. It's how most of us have been trained.

While having the right team of professionals to treat and advise me was absolutely necessary, I learned that my own self-awareness and keen instinct were crucial for achieving wellness.

Having the confidence to know I am the best judge of my personal needs and limitations—in particular, of what I can and cannot do work-wise—remains central to ensuring my ongoing mental health. My path to wellness has not been a straight or a smooth one. And I continue to encounter potential pitfalls and unforeseen challenges from time to time. But by keeping my senses sharp and attuned to any uneasiness within, even when I don't quite understand the reason for the discomfort, I can usually abort a potential trigger. I have successfully sidestepped several likely backslides, as a result of paying close attention to my "un-wellness" radar.

I have met people who have experienced mental health issues such as anxiety or severe stress response but either don't possess the self-knowledge to identify their triggers and how they might counteract them or, if they do know where the hairline cracks are in their own foundation, they seem to lack a strong enough voice to express their personal boundaries. They might be caught in a web of old childhood or family beliefs, especially ones tied to their unworthiness, and this inhibits them from valuing their right to expression and to mental health.

I feel sad for those individuals, because without the ability to set limits for themselves, they run the risk of triggering a more serious response, one when the mind and body together decide to nullify the threat, in whatever way possible. This could take the form of severe generalized anxiety, depression, or panic attacks (events described as "the universe running you into a brick wall" by my sister Lorraine). I believe such a dramatic event can occur when a more "reasonable" approach is continually overlooked by the conscious mind, leaving the unconscious mind to choose how to ensure self-preservation.

Witnessing someone hit that wall is not fun for anyone; having it happen to you is even less so. But it is sometimes the only option left for our psyche when we insist on maintaining the familiar yet unhealthy *status quo*. Unfortunately, it is sometimes the only way for people to give themselves permission to look after their own needs. We tend to look elsewhere for permission when we should really be looking inside ourselves.

I am grateful to have inherited a ready-for-battle attitude from my mother, which has served me well in taking a stand with and for myself. Taking a stand within myself was the first and most demanding step for standing up and getting healthy.

PIVOTAL POINTS

There were pivotal points in my journey that changed the game for me. Their importance was such that, had any one of them not occurred, I would be telling a quite different story.

1. I learned that even good things can cause anxiety (and potential relapse) and that there really can be too much of a good thing. I learned that for me, balance must always be at the forefront of my mind, in all things.

2. My family doctor laid it out quite simply. I had three choices and I needed to pick one:

- Keep my job and continue with increasing depression events.
- Quit my job and eliminate what triggered my illness (my work environment).
- Change how I think about my work environment so I could return.

This seemingly obvious decision path gave me my power back; I had put the illness in charge of my future, but my doctor helped me to see that I was still in charge, that I had a choice.

I eventually chose the third option by flipping my thoughts and envisioning what I needed to get from work in addition to a paycheck. I say *eventually,* because my first decision had been to quit my job and taste what freedom from the shackles felt like, and it was delicious.

3. I found a medication that worked for me. What a thrill it was to rediscover my personality! I literally hadn't been myself in more than twenty years.

4. One more thing I learned from cognitive behavior therapy: Just because you think it doesn't mean it's true; and just because you feel it doesn't make it true, either. This opened my mind and helped put the controls back where they belonged, in my capable hands.

Resources
My Joyful Life Action Plan

We must create an action plan, ideally while we are feeling well, so we have something trusted to latch onto when we are unwell.

1. Replace negative thoughts with neutral thinking. Situations don't have to be black or white.
2. Be creative. Indulge your soul and make meaningful use of your hands.
3. Establish a daily routine with a positive focus.
4. Connect with Spirit every day, ideally at a regular time as part of your routine.
5. See personal discipline in a positive light. It's powerful for you. Find small ways to employ self-discipline and notice how it uplifts your mood.
6. Exercise self-care every day; you know best what you need, and you deserve the care.
7. Regularly visualize your best self, with intention. You can become that person.
8. Exercise at least three times per week for thirty to forty minutes.
9. Spend time in nature especially where there are mature trees, running water, or mountains if you are lucky enough to live close by.
10. Connect with people. Social contact is critical for being well and staying well.

11. Create a "High-Five" book to compliment yourself and record your progress. (A written high-five to yourself, so to speak.) Only you know what warrants noting and only you need to see your book—make it as joyful as you can!

12. If you feel stuck, write down a plan (even the start of a plan will do) to get you moving again. Take charge of your wellness.

13. Lastly, be kind and gentle with yourself; treat yourself as you would your dearest friend.

PROBLEM-SOLVING PROCESS

When things go wrong or I am faced with a problem, rather than panic, I attempt to apply the problem-solving process, which I learned from my CBT doctor/therapist:

1. Identify the problem.
2. Gather information on the problem or situation.
3. Generate alternatives (options).
4. Choose one.
5. Do it.
6. Evaluate it.

While applying the above process, practice transforming your negative thoughts into neutral ones; once you have mastered neutral thinking, try to further transform them into positive thoughts. One step at a time!

LIST OF DOS AND DON'TS

DO	DON'T
Set achievable goals.	Wait for things to happen or change.
Reward yourself for your achievements.	Focus on disappointments.
Simplify or change goals that are not working for you.	Get stuck continuing with goals that you find frustrating.
Make plans for your free time.	Sit around with nothing to do.
Regularly review your goals and achievements.	Catastrophize.
Make contact with friends at least once a week (preferably more often).	Isolate yourself when feeling down.
Discuss and share the positive parts of your life with friends.	Focus too much on the negative.
Be consistent with your daily schedule (i.e., regular and reasonable bedtime and rising time).	Just "float" through your day, letting your mood dictate your schedule.
Seek out and initiate pleasant activities and events.	Get stuck in a routine that does not serve you and allow you opportunity to enjoy life.
Stay aware of automatic thoughts that affect your mood; try to correct these thoughts if you can.	Let negative automatic thinking go unchallenged.

Don't feel you need to do all of the above right away—take one at a time; you don't want to exacerbate feelings of being overwhelmed. Think of these dos and don'ts as part of your action plan for developing healthy skills over time as a precaution against relapse.

We hear a lot about balance, especially work-life balance, so much so that it has lost much of its substance. Most people would agree that it's a nice thing to have in our sights, but for me, balance is critical. I can't function without it.

While balance in all areas of my life is the goal, I accept that this ideal is not always possible all of the time. However, I especially guard those certain areas that are essential for me: creativity and spirituality. They *must* have a strong place in my daily life.

Healthy eating and sleeping are important things for the body, and they help me in managing migraines.

Connecting with good people is important for my mind and my spirit. I wouldn't have thought that having friends was necessary for my health, but depression taught me that it is so.

Before depression knocked me off my feet, I had few friends and didn't put much thought into it. As a working mom, I was busy and I found it hard to make friends anyway. I was more self-conscious than I cared to acknowledge—it's only in hindsight that I see that.

I often felt that I had nothing in common with most of the people I met socially because I lived so much in my head. I often felt unworthy of their company and didn't pursue budding friendships, believing it wasn't worth the hassle. I told myself I didn't want or need friends because I had so many hobbies to keep me company. It took me some time to understand the value of having friends—not to mention the importance of *being* a friend. I am so thankful for having learned that lesson, because my friends enrich my life in a way I can't express. (You know who you are, and I *love* each one of you!)

"Authentic power. It happens when purpose aligns with personality to serve the greater good."
—Oprah Winfrey

Balancing a life must be learned and practiced; it is not an automatic thing. Maintaining balance takes discipline and self-respect—self-respect for helping to identify those things that are important for *you,* and discipline for ensuring that you make it happen for yourself and continue to do so. It sometimes calls for a lifestyle change.

My personal balance is unique to me, and yours will look different from mine or a friend's. We each create our own recipe for what constitutes good balance in our lives. If you are feeling out of balance, it might be a call to review your current activities and perhaps reconfigure some of the bits that made life go out of kilter.

The Importance of Balance

Thankfully, I am now able to manage most of my triggers for depression and anxiety by keeping balance in my life.

For the work-specific triggers, it's my job to ensure that my manager has a clear understanding of my needs and limitations and that she understands and accepts her role as my sometimes-protector from the minefields of potential triggers. She is also my coach for dealing effectively with certain colleagues known to hold live charges for me. This, too, is a balancing act—one for which clear and ongoing communication is essential.

My previous manager understood what work I could and could not do. If she wasn't sure, she knew to ask me and have a discussion about it. It was my job to become aware of my internal responses and to communicate that information to her. Together for three years, we built a mutually trusting relationship.

But because change is ever present, learning to navigate through evolving circumstances is also part of staying healthy, especially for someone with depression and anxiety (whose first response might be to run rather than learn healthy coping mechanisms).

This balance was severely tested when my manager retired and I found myself reporting to someone new. Despite having initiated a three-way meeting with both managers to discuss my circumstance, the transition to a new manager was rough. Happily, our working relationship improved quickly and I can now simply chalk up an initial, unfortunate experience to a rough start. No more and no less. All normal.

The experience did confirm, however, that knowing *about* managing an employee with mental health issues (which many managers have been exposed to from attending a one-day workshop offered by my organization) and *doing* it are not the same thing. Not at all.

In addition to keeping my manager apprised of my mental health temperature, I try to keep my colleagues informed of major changes, as well. I recall asking to speak at one of our section meetings to inform them that I was on the edge of relapse and had entered into crisis-management mode.

I introduced the topic by giving a brief history of my depression, because only a few in attendance were aware of my struggle, and went on to explain that I was working with our manager to determine what work I would drop for the time being and what new tasks I would take on as part of an altered workplace accommodation.

Their response was compassionate; they wanted to know how they could help. I told them their willingness to hear what I needed was already helping. I thanked them for their support, and we moved on to the next item on the agenda. I was very pleased with their reception and felt better and stronger having told them.

I have always been open about my mental health problems. I feel it's better to keep my colleagues informed of changes rather than having them wonder about my performance—or non-performance, as the case may be—and letting them fill in their own information where they see gaps. That is what people will do. They will make up their own stories—often not the most flattering ones, either.

It's important that I feel safe in my environment; without that, fear and anxiety can and do take over my world and lead me straight to falling apart. And I never want to return to that dreadful pit called depression.

It is worth repeating that learning to maintain balance takes conscious effort, planning, and lots of discipline: being present through mindfulness; planning for solitude and stillness in my day and week, a time when I can connect with the Divine, my source, and ground myself; and focusing on keeping my energy vibrating high, healthily, and positively.

With a chronic anxiety condition, when too much is happening in my life, whether or not I have control over it, it can cause me to become overwhelmed and can make it very hard to get back on track. I feel as though I get sucked into a vortex or a treadmill of a zillion things that need my attention, right now. I find it difficult to focus or make choices, to prioritize what to work on next. I get pulled into the work one hundred percent and have difficulty letting go of that mental stronghold and focusing on other things in order to achieve balance.

Sometimes, I need to take a step back and away from activity, to spend time rebalancing with the right side of the brain, with intuition, spirit, and creativity. And I must consciously spend time relaxing my mind.

Within balance, success is mine; outside it, I crash and burn.

I continue to learn skills to protect myself and to better manage my world—because my life depends on it.

About Stigma

What is stigma? A compilation of dictionary definitions reveals that it is "a mark of disgrace associated with a particular circumstance, quality, or person's character," and gives the following example: "The stigma of having gone to prison will always be with me."

But why should there be shame, disgrace, humiliation, or embarrassment associated with an illness? The stigma is very real, and I believe it stems from fear and a lack of understanding—from not knowing how to manage or have a discussion about depression.

I am doing what I can to raise awareness of mental illness and the value of mental health. And that starts by sharing my own story with anyone who shows interest. I am not a famous person with a public profile that demands attention, but my story is no less real and valid. As someone with lived experience of a mental illness, I have a role to play in the battle to debunk the stigma that weighs heavily on those touched by the illness—whether as victims, survivors, or their friends and family.

"It's better to be kind than right. We don't need a brilliant mind that speaks, but a patient heart who listens."
—Anonymous

If you don't think the stigma is real, perhaps it's because you haven't experienced it first-hand, and that's understandable. But have you spoken recently with the spouse or family member of someone who died of suicide? I'm thinking of the one who refuses to publish an obituary for fear that "people will know," or, if the notice of death is written vaguely enough to skirt the actual cause of death, people might telephone the house wanting to know about the circumstances. And they'll need to be told or lied to. Even if they don't voice it, callers might hold the closest survivors somehow responsible.

Some relatives feel it's better (or more comfortable) to ignore the death altogether, to treat the suicide in a way that perhaps mimics how the individual might have felt during his or her life: invisible and unworthy.

On the other hand, some families of suicide are helping to fight the stigma by speaking out. I commend them for turning a highly traumatic and sad occurrence into something that could help those who are troubled by mental illness today, or who will be in the future.

Do you remember hearing about the "C" word or the "big C"? That's what we used to call cancer a few decades ago because the word was too emotionally loaded to be spoken aloud. Older generations sometimes still use that term, perhaps out of habit or a lingering discomfort.

It was through publicly raising awareness over many years that the unmentionable started to take in air. It was by everyday people gaining notice in the public arena through acts of courage and using their own illness to raise funds for research. It was as a result of high-profile fundraising campaigns that the stigma eventually faded, coupled with an increasing number of success stories from people who beat the disease thanks in large part to funded research.

This opening of thought is beginning to happen concerning mental illness. In Canada, we are raising awareness about it locally and nationally through media and publicity campaigns; by establishing the Canadian Mental Health Commission; by employers like the Ontario Public Service declaring 2014 the Year of Mental Health; by public figures speaking out about their personal struggles with mental illness; and by people like you and me talking about it and sharing our stories. In this fight, the little person can have a huge impact by being the change she wants to see in her community.

Because mental illness is an invisible condition, some are quietly opting to mark their bodies with semi-colon tattoos, often on the wrist, as a way of reaching out and opening conversations with other survivors, their friends, and their families.

The symbol signifies that mental illness need not be a permanent sentence, ending with a finite period. It can end with a semi-colon and be an unfinished sentence, allowing for more of the person's story to unfold.

The current estimate is that 20 percent of Canadians suffer from severe depression (that's one in five people!) and fewer than 6 percent ever receive treatment. I like this quote by Brian Day, MD, former president of the Canadian Medical Association, which produced these numbers: "[the stigma of mental illness is the] final frontier of socially acceptable discrimination."

Part of the divergence is due to the stigma that mental illness carries, and part is because we don't know where to find help.

We haven't grown up knowing these things. It is something we need to learn. Thanks to programs like Mental Health First Aid, making its way into the Western Hemisphere and being offered through an increasing number of workplaces and communities, our society is slowly learning about these things. Education is the only way out.

ACCEPTANCE TAKES TIME

Self-stigma was a huge hurdle for me, because I felt undeserving—undeserving of happiness, undeserving of having work that I enjoyed, undeserving of a fulfilling life.

And I felt unworthy. I experienced what I have heard described as Imposter Syndrome, feeling surrounded by super-competent people, all much better than I. I found myself forever lacking. I felt unworthy of being loved, that I was just taking up space. Somewhere along the way, I had lost my purpose. I perceived myself as having unreasonable expectations that could never be satisfied, and I wasn't able to lower my expectations, either. No matter how hard I tried, I could never be happy.

I had struggled with this weight strapped to my solar plexus since my early teens. Having children brought some respite from my dissatisfaction (because I loved mothering), but even that was temporary; as a stay-at-home mom, I soon felt isolated and unworthy in that arena too, and I yearned to find value from the business world, then the nonprofit good-causes world, and finally I hoped to find it in the for-the-public-good government world. While this final stop did bring about my breakdown, it also helped me to crack the riddle of life—how to feel fulfilled and happy.

In 2010, I began working hard at changing my self-image to better reflect the reality that others saw in me and that I eventually came to see in myself. My husband helped me on this journey to self-acceptance by helping me to accept my illness and to see the person I had become.

I took the time to grieve over the loss of those years when the illness was at its worst. One fine day, as Robert and I sat in our field on what we called the shade shelter, observing the wind as it played with the tall grasses in the surrounding farm fields, I apologized for having put him through those agonizing years. Though he felt my words were unnecessary because it was the illness and not me who was responsible, my heart needed to apologize. Being the gallant man that he is, Robert accepted my apology. It is what my soul needed, and I felt a release from the process.

Grieving allowed me to let go of the past and accept the present. I will never forget those "lost" years, and honestly, it's better that I don't. You see, the memory protects me from the worst of the illness.

I can't control how others respond when they learn that I have depression, but I can help them to better understand my experience of it. I also can teach them how I want to be treated—with consideration and respect, the same as everyone else.

My illness and I have evolved to where I can now harness my disability—I use it to help shine a light on mental illness and to help to lift the stigma. And perhaps, if I am at the right place at the right time, along with Spirit's guidance, I will help someone out there who is buried under his or her own struggles. My deepest desire is to help someone see hope for himself or herself. Hope is something we all need.

My illness taught me…
- to develop and express my voice
- to recognize when it's time to reach out
- to know what is worth fighting for
- to grow my compassion for others
- that I am my own specialist and advocate
- that true acceptance takes time and patience
- that friends are necessary for my health
- that grieving has a place in the healing process
- most important, that I am a happier person because of my illness.

A Lesson from Peru

I spent two months in 2008 volunteering for Awamaki, a nonprofit organization that supports weaving cooperatives of indigenous women located in rural villages in the highlands of Peru. These communities practice traditional, back-strap weaving and help to support their families with the sales. I put my talents to use there by developing product designs that incorporate the artisans' weaving, in an effort to broaden the appeal and expand their reach. I created samples and sewing patterns that could later be fabricated by the women themselves using regular sewing machines on their premises. I was pleased to contribute to such a worthy cause. And what I learned while there will serve me for a lifetime.

The project allowed me to experience what true joy and contentment feels like and to enjoy the beauty of marrying talent with work. And I determined to get some more of that once back in Canada. I knew I was meant to be productive in a creative space. I felt I had unlocked the secret to my happiness and that I had been created to do nothing less.

I could feel Mama Bear's power inside of me, joyfully radiating from my every pore. I spent most days inside of my power while in Peru, shining my light and discovering my inner beauty. I was gleeful, a fully content, peaceful, happy, and joyfully creative woman, engaged with her community. It was heaven on earth.

I recall a scene one clear morning near the end of my Peruvian sojourn, the fog at Machu Picchu having completely lifted. I was walking away from the Sun Gate where I had stopped for a rest and snack and I was ambling down the cobbled path by myself with no one else on the trail, when a sudden wave of warmth filled and lifted my heart and I knew this was as good as it gets! It was the first time I had experienced such purity of joy.

I had to find a way to connect with that treasure once back home, because my soul's very essence depended on it. Now that I had tasted it, I felt I would die without it.

When I was six years old and in first grade at a Catholic school in Northern Ontario, my teacher told the class that each of us was born with a special talent that was uniquely ours and that it was our job while here on earth to grow that talent, that we were not to return to God with our talent undeveloped. It was clear in my child's mind that I would need to become an artist, because my talent was in drawing and coloring. There was no doubt in my young mind, because everyone just knew it was my talent—the other kids, my teacher, and my friends. I'm not sure what my family thought of my abilities, because my siblings were even more creatively talented than I, the youngest of five at the time.

I returned from Peru eager to try the small business route, selling my creations online and at craft shows. I began making cuddly, warm winter coats and sold a few of these. Then I crafted one-of-a-kind jackets, vests, and tote bags accented with hand-weaving from Peru. And finally, I attempted to launch MaBelle, my one-person workroom for custom drapes and window treatments.

While none of these business ventures took hold in the end, I certainly have no regrets about testing these ideas because of the lessons they afforded me. Having instead made the choice to finish my career at my government job, I am hugely thankful to have retired with a pension that can support my creative hands.

On Talent and Old Beliefs

Growing up in a family of artistic siblings, I thought that having drawing ability was normal, because it was present in every-thing that we did. I also believed that I was far less talented than my brother and four sisters, because they were *really* talented in my estimation. (My younger sister, Louise, would arrive seven years after me to bring the count to six.)

As the youngest, it made perfect sense that my abilities would be less developed than my siblings', but that fact didn't occur to my young mind; I just knew I was forever trying to catch up and imitate whatever they were doing. This meant I didn't develop my own creative voice until well into adulthood.

Another belief I grew up with was that seeking work that called for artistic talent was foolhardy, unrealistic, and plain dumb. In my family, it was an accepted fact that no one could make a living with art and the only artists out there were the starving ones. The decision to ignore any artistic field for a career was made long before I was of an age to be considering these things. I knew only that my work life wouldn't have anything to do with art—not architecture, not graphic design, not drafting, not interior design, not even organizing art events. How unfortunate.

In actuality, my family didn't discuss careers of any kind. We had a very short view of life, based on the realities of living on the poverty line and sometimes below it. The goal was to get a job and make enough money to pay the rent and eat. And that's as broad as my view got in those days. From what I can gather, the same was true for most of my siblings.

Many years later, having gone through some periods of significant depression, I was compelled to do some serious soul-searching. I finally figured out that it wasn't the talent that was lacking in me. Not at all. What I had been missing all along was self-esteem. I inherited a frail self-esteem and inadvertently built up the wrong self-image. Ah, I was at the crux of it now!

Over the years from my childhood to the present, this breach in my foundation had not found new strength. On the contrary, the psychological weakness had just permeated into more areas of my life. It needed a makeover so that its power could be realigned to its proper position—where it was controlled by me, not me by it.

Okay, I need to strengthen my self-esteem and rebrand my self-image, I thought, *I can do that!* This was good, because then I had something concrete to focus on, something to get my teeth into. The task appealed to my action-oriented personality. Until I stopped to think. *Uh... now, how does one go about doing that exactly?* How could I reverse the image I carried of myself, when my self-esteem was virtually non-existent?

I could not afford to spend $100 an hour for a therapist. This would be a long-term effort over months and perhaps years. I didn't have that kind of money, so I made up my own method, and it worked for me and my circumstances.

As is wise when launching chartless endeavors, I started small, by documenting the tiniest of successes until they became greater in number. I built upon these until my successes broadened and took on a more significant stature. Eventually, I was able to observe my successes and capture a more realistic picture of myself.

Today, I believe I have a healthy sense of my creative abilities and qualities, while keeping well within the boundaries of humility and good taste. And I know what I am capable of creating—anything I so desire!

I don't remember how I came up with this strategy. I suspect it must have been through reading and listening to inspiring audiobooks and web-based radio shows.

The fourth belief that I learned early in life—and this is

one I am keeping, because it's a good one—is that I can do anything I set my mind to. When I am feeling well, there is no obstacle I cannot surmount or get around. My mom taught me that. As a single parent of six rambunctious and "creative" kids (read: what interesting and original mess can we get up to now?), she was the most resourceful and self-reliant person I have ever known. She taught me that if I wanted something that we couldn't afford (which was most things), I should just go ahead and make something like it. In my house, being bored was seen as a reflection of a lack of ingenuity, of which I learned by example to develop plenty.

When I was nine years old, my mom made me the most beautiful magenta-colored pants from the satin lining of an old fur coat (at a time when up-cycling wasn't a thing!). We certainly couldn't afford to buy fabric, and besides, no stores were open at the late hour that she came home from the evening shift working the switchboard of a local motel. That is when she found my scribbled note explaining that I *needed* clean pants to wear to school the next day, as a treat instead of the usual school uniform. She knew that my only pants, which I wore for playing outside, would never do. So, she stayed up all night cutting out and sewing my rich-kid pants. I was never so proud to go to school as I was wearing those beautiful, tailor-made pants. (Thanks, Mom!)

My Thinking Capacity

One of the nasty things about having depression is that while the illness is in flare-up mode, you are deprived of the very thing you need to help yourself: your thinking abilities. Because the brain is not firing at full capacity during these periods, it becomes difficult to convey accurate information on your state of being—for example, in updating your boss, your spouse, or your friends, or in filling out notoriously long and complex forms for insurance purposes.

Ironically, as my condition began to improve, it became clear to me—because I could think a bit better then—that I couldn't fully trust my own thinking. It wasn't that I would engage in manic or unpredictable thoughts, but that I couldn't gauge things properly. I couldn't be sure when it was time to discuss a change in medication with my doctor. I was never sure if my self-assessment, from my insider's viewpoint, was accurate, and if it was similar to what I presented on the outside. How did my "inside experience" compare to my husband's experience when interacting with me? I trusted his opinion but not my own. Because the illness was affecting the very part used in processing thought, I felt at a great disadvantage. I never felt that people fully understood this dilemma.

Perhaps this deficiency is one reason why I was more adept at sensing insights with my intuition rather than thinking something through, and why I was able to rely on my intuition so thoroughly. It was probably my best asset.

• • • EXERCISE • • •

Setting Your Personal Boundaries

This exercise, from a workshop with Sonia Choquette, is great to do anytime, but especially in the morning as a way to set the intention for your day.

I find the actions especially useful when I feel like I am being encroached upon by people who sap up my energy, when I find them crossing over into my personal space more than I like, and when I find myself more concerned with their issues/topics/needs than my own. When I first returned to work, I felt quite vulnerable and used this technique to protect myself from encroaching energies. I needed to focus on establishing my emotional boundaries. This exercise enabled me to be in my power in a quiet and sure way.

- Standing in the center of your space, take five or six deep and calming breaths to center yourself.
- Raise your arms wide, palms open and facing out in front of you, as if you are pushing a wall out. Stretch those arms and push forward.
- While speaking, "I will not be stuck between a rock and a hard place," now push with your hands to the right of you.
- Repeat as above, this time with your hands to the left of you.
- With hands facing down, push down the personal history and whatever is keeping you stuck—push down the rising tide.
- Raise up your arms and push as if to raise the ceiling.
- Turn around, flicking the imaginary stuff off your shoulders, telling any monkeys to get off your back.
- End with a "spiritual burp": pound your fist to the heart chakra and expel the sound "HA!" in a strong voice.
- Enjoy your day!

A number of people supported me during my get-well
year and beyond—doctors with medical perspectives, a
homoeopathic doctor and acupuncturist, massage therapist,
chiropractic doctor, and specialists with psychological interests.
Most important were my two closest supports, my husband,
Robert, and my dear friend, Sue Scott.

I kept them all in the loop in terms of my progress, challenges, and setbacks. I would discuss my thinking with Robert
and Sue, sometimes together and sometimes alone, and I gave
them permission to discuss my case in my absence. I trusted
them completely and knew they wanted what was best for me.
In fact, I trusted their thinking above my own and I needed their
help with moving my healing forward.

I was tested for food sensitivities and allergies and made
changes to my diet accordingly. I included quality nutritional
supplements as prescribed, to support healthy brain function
and stress response.

I am grateful for the contribution that each of these people
made to my recovery and for supporting me in my healing
journey.

When I returned to work, I included my managers as part of
my support team, because their mutual trust and commitment to

my success was paramount. I don't believe I could have successfully managed the work, and the work environment, without
the engagement of a supportive manager—and I had three such
managers over the years.

RETURNING TO WORK

The World Health Organization (in its report titled "When
The Time Is Right for Going Back to
Work," Geneva, 2000) recommends
establishing a multidisciplinary team
for each individual that is unique to
that person, to bring about a syner-
gistic partnership among the employee,
employer, health professionals, unions,
and insurance companies.

"When I gave
you My Spirit, I
empowered you
to live beyond
your natural ability
and strength."

—Sarah Young

Centered on the employee and a
shared desire for a successful and lasting work reintegration,
they suggest that this team can include the following:

• Family doctor
• Psychiatrist and/or psychotherapist often using cognitive
behavior therapy
• Vocational consultant (or occupational therapist)
• Union (or other advocate if in a non-unionized environment)
• Employer
• Insurance company

I tried to establish such a team for my own final return to work,
with limited success. My workplace did not have a system in
place that allowed for this type of multidisciplinary support;
there was no team in their return-to-work concept.

In my place of work, managers have access to a mental health
specialist to assist them in navigating the established system for

dealing with an employee with mental health problems that affect his or her job performance. But employees don't enjoy the same access. Any discussion regarding accommodation of needs and/or limitations is done with the manager. In my experience, there was never a time when the three of us met to discuss options or specific concerns. I found that limitation frustrating.

Employees can access a therapist for five or six sessions through the Employee Assistance Program (EAP), but the therapist deals only with the employee; he or she is not given an opportunity to contribute to the thinking and planning with the manager regarding the employee and workplace accommodation. Another missed opportunity.

At no time does the system permit a conversation between the manager and the employee's doctor, therapist, or other specialist to take place; all contact is done through formal letters and a question-and-answer format. And if the manager is not satisfied with the answers provided, she can opt to have the employee reassessed by another specialist selected from the employer's list of qualified professionals. (My understanding is that this option is typically activated when the employee is seen as not cooperating.) The employee gets to recount her story from the beginning yet again, this time to a total stranger who is being paid by the employer. And if the employee's mental illness happens to be depression or generalized anxiety, you can imagine that such a scenario might not help matters. What a perfect opportunity for the staffer to re-experience emotional trauma and "enjoy" heightened anxiety. Yes, it can be a frustrating system for the employee and perhaps for the manager as well. But enough about that!

My medical leave was due to end soon and I was reluctant to return to work even though I desperately wanted to be employed. I was scared of the workplace environment, afraid that I would not be capable of functioning, that I would get sucked up by feelings regarding the futility of it all, the sense that I was fighting an upstream battle through an unproductive process, and becoming overwhelmed by it all. Again. I was scared of being sent into relapse (for a fourth time). I felt fragile and raw and without personal defenses, like a newborn baby wholly dependent on others for its survival.

Ever so slowly, I realized that I alone could not change this large beast of an organization that employed me, and that I had better work on changing myself instead, or else I would be unsuccessful in returning to work and I would find myself unemployed and without resources.

As I mentioned earlier, during a visit to my CBT doctor/therapist, she advised that I needed to change my attitude toward my workplace to better cope with my frustrations. I don't recall any suggestion as to how I should go about doing this. I arrived home from the appointment feeling defeated by the lack of tools for accomplishing what sounded more like a cliché than a solution.

How the heck was I supposed to change what I thought of my workplace, an opinion that I had built up over twenty years and considered to be the truth? I saw my thinking as central to my very being, to my personality, to who I was as a person.

I didn't believe I would ever be able to accept the organization as something other than how I viewed it because my feelings were so definite. But the thought never left my mind. I began to wonder what would happen if I did have a different mindset and what that might look like. I would probably need to let go of a few things: my perfectionist tendencies, my expectation that work should be meaningful, the belief that the intelligent and dedicated people who made up the organization should be capable of designing effective processes and procedures, that since the employees comprised the organization, we should be willing and skilled enough to do our work in a respectful and kind manner. We should be able to turn it around.

I would need to let go of these beliefs and create new ones, ones that would serve me better and protect me from my deep-rooted fears and expectations. My priority needed to be self-preservation. I needed to put my wellness first, ahead of the organization's desires or demands, and ahead of my own personal expectations.

I started by asking my deepest self what it needed in order to feel okay within that work environment. Through a mental process that involved visualization and analysis of the different tasks in my job, seeing and feeling myself doing the tasks, while paying close attention to how my mind and body responded, I determined that my core job—which involved leading corporate initiatives across all divisions within the organization—did not suit my temperament.

I took it a step further. Still using visualization as the primary tool, I was able to isolate specific tasks within my job that I did enjoy and was good at (creating internal communication for a website; editing documents by taking complex messaging and making it more easily accessible using clear structure and language).

Then, I began to research what type of work might suit me better. I looked at job ads from a variety of workplaces, searching for a better fit. I investigated retraining options and looked into teaching as a possibility. I wanted to teach sewing skills to junior-high students (I knew an acquaintance who had this job, and it sounded perfect for me). But the "domestic skills" program had been phased out by most school boards in the province, so I was not too hopeful on that front.

> "No one can make you feel inferior without your consent."
> —Eleanor Roosevelt

My next choice was to teach young children in French-language schools, even if it meant moving out of our English-speaking area. I went so far as to write an exam and be interviewed for a condensed and intensive online teacher-training program. The coordinator had my in-class placement ready before I was even enrolled for the training, let alone graduated! They were that desperate for French-speaking teachers. This was a high-demand discipline, which was good for my prospects.

I thought I could juggle the teacher program while still working at my job. In hindsight, I know I could not have sustained the grueling pace that awaited me, given my low tolerance for stress of any kind. But I was determined to leave a job where I felt useless and stuck. Planning my escape was all I could think of.

I also investigated jobs in other ministries within the larger organization, especially those that involved direct contact with clients, thinking this would satisfy my desire for purpose and meaning in my work. I job-shadowed a colleague in Ottawa who was a public guardian serving a caseload of vulnerable adults. Although I greatly admired her role, after spending three days on the job with her, I felt that being on call and making daily decisions on behalf of those with special needs, dealing with their issues and problems all day long, would not support my own need for minimal stress, predictability, and having control over my day.

As for my home-based drapery business idea, I estimated that it probably would bring in the equivalent to earning minimum wage, at least to start. But it would offer no health benefits, no paid vacations, no supports, and no backup. Talk about inviting stress into my life! I am thankful I saw the light on that idea before going too far. I only had to misplace an order (for a window in our own house, which I designed and constructed as if for a client) to understand how utterly stressed and anxious I could become if this were my true business. Again, this idea was born from a desperate need to flee what experience was telling me was an unhealthy and scary work environment.

It took me a full year of working on deep healing to feel mentally and emotionally ready to return to work. I felt better equipped and hopeful that all I had learned would serve me well, that it would help me not only in being a productive employee but especially in staying well while there. I had six and a half more years to go before I could retire with a pension.

• • • EXERCISE • • •

Creating Your Support Team

You must build your own network. These are people in your life that you would like to have as formal supporters. Determine exactly how you would like them to help (babysitting or petsitting to give you time to yourself, weekly get-togethers to prepare meals or bake, enjoying long nature walks) and make your request.

Have challenges in common. It's great to have at least one person in your group who has gone through the same thing as you. You will be able to share things with this person that others might not understand.

Avoid relying on only one person for support. When the going gets tough for you, you will probably need more support than one person can give. It's best to keep some limits on how much help you will ask of each person.

Keep up your own efforts. Though your support team can provide help, it cannot take on the problem for you. You need to do what you can to help yourself as well (exercise, eat healthy, set goals for yourself, mark your progress, and celebrate even small successes). Supports can drift away if they sense that they are working harder on your difficulty than you are.

Mood Emergency Action Plan

Having a plan in case your mood worsens can assist you in getting help quickly and perhaps reduce the length and depth of the bad patch.

1. **Increase your rewards.** When your mood declines, it is important for you to take extra care of yourself. List those things that you could do to build up the enjoyable side of your life, even when you don't much feel like having fun. You need to be specific. For example, my plan might include:

    a. Plan a weekend away, preferably in nature.

    b. Visit with friends—list them by name.

    c. Buy knitting and sewing magazines.

    d. Hang out in a fabric store; buy some bright samples.

e. Go out for lunch with positive people—name them.

f. Offer to petsit for a friend's dog or cat, and then cuddle the pet like crazy!

2. **Reduce obligations.** When your mood is in decline, you are less able to handle a lot of obligations. Like a hot air balloon, you will want to let go of a few sandbags when you feel yourself sinking. For example:

a. Don't plan and prepare meals every day—ready-made meals are fine right now.

b. Meet with your manager and make a plan to reduce your stress and responsibilities at work.

c. Plan a reserve fund to cover costs of occasional house-cleaning and babysitting help.

What other things would reduce your load in a mood emergency? What would you need to do in advance to make that possible?

3. **Get professional help.** The longer a problem goes without attention, the bigger it will feel and the deeper the struggle to get yourself out of it.

a. Keep your list of caregivers (your physician, therapist, others) with their phone numbers in a safe place that is easy to remember.

b. Give permission to one or two close friends or family members to tell you when you should seek help. Sometimes they can see this better than you can for yourself.

c. To prepare, before you end your contact with your therapist, ask if you can bypass the waitlist and get back to treatment quickly if the need arises.

d. Should things get worse, how could you get professional help quickly? List your ideas and people to talk to:

_____

_____

_____

_____

_____

e. Get support. In the event of a major mood decline, you will need the support of others. You might just want to talk with them, or you might ask them to do specific things such as taking you to do your groceries. What type of support would be helpful? How would you arrange for this in advance? List individual names with contact information:

_____

_____

_____

_____

_____

4. **Manage your lifestyle.** What are you doing to replenish your energy? Are you getting enough physical activity? Maintain a regular sleep regimen by going to bed and getting up at a reasonable hour. Watch your sugar and caffeine intake; they make the stress response more active, and that's the last thing you need. One of the most important factors in caring for yourself is maintaining an adequate social network. What are the most important things for you to enhance? Have fun! Especially when your mood is going for a dive, fun is not optional. It is important!

My leave time was not an opportunity to goof off and still get a paycheck. I was off work because I couldn't cope with doing my job. I was deficient and ill-equipped to do the work I used to do. I was on medical leave for an indeterminate length of time, in the hope that I could heal and return to work feeling "all better." I had been in a similar situation twice before, so I knew the drill—and it worried me, because the other times didn't offer permanent healing, only temporary reprieves from a debilitating depression. My brain had never returned to a pre-depression healthy state (the way I had expected), nor would it. I knew this from the reading I had done over the years, that the brain is physically changed by undergoing depression. I was not to expect the old brain back. I accepted that and focused on the present.

I needed some structure in my days, something predictable for me to hang on to. My mind was the furthest thing from stable— it was scared, discouraged, and badly in need of someone or something to lead it away from the edge of the abyss.

Perfectly Yourself: 9 Lessons for Enduring Happiness by Matthew Kelly provided a foundation for building my own structure and daily discipline. As soon as I saw the structure presented in the book, I knew that I wanted that, and that I had to create this for myself.

I remembered a phone conversation I had had years ago with my sister Sylvia. I was in my mid-twenties and she would have been in her early thirties. She was job-hunting and was quite interested in an opportunity to work with a local cinematography company. She was interested in photography at the time and was excited by the idea of working with a bunch of creative people. She also relished the freedom that, in her view, flexible hours would provide, and she loved not feeling hemmed in by a nine-to-five job; she hated having structure imposed on her life. Sylvia is what I would call a free spirit.

> "Kindness toward ourselves precedes all genuine and lasting growth."
> —Matthew Kelly

I listened to her explain the appeal of this type of intensive job, one that was dictated by the creative process rather than by arbitrary work hours, a job that would demand long hours but in return would offer the freedom of having several days off in a row when the work was done.

I thought to myself, *As for me, I quite like the nine-to-five structure.* The thought of not knowing when quitting time was did not appeal to me, of not being able to plan activities or take an evening course for social connection, in case of work demands. I especially liked having a regular paycheck each week. We were certainly different in what made us feel good—I liked security while she preferred freedom.

This little thought born thirty years earlier helped me to understand that I needed to inject structure into my wide-open days; I somehow knew that it was paramount to getting me to the other, brighter side of this current "episode." When in a depressive state, it can be difficult, sometimes impossible, to know what you want or need.

While structure was by no means all I needed, I knew that whatever I *did* need—once I figured that out—would only benefit from fitting into a daily structure and personal discipline.

Perfectly Yourself offered me that structure. It helped me to understand that structure was something that I not only needed, but that I desired.

I approached my sabbatical life as a project and I was to be the project manager, like a runner training for a marathon or a student researching and defending a thesis. It undoubtedly would be a long haul and could work only if I tackled one manageable piece at a time, bit by bit and day by day. The job of getting me better could overwhelm me otherwise.

A Road Map

Thankfully, I came across *Perfectly Yourself* early in my "sabbatical" year. It was on January 2, 2010, to be precise. I recently came across the receipt, and it brought me back to that prophetic day. This book all but jumped into my hands as I browsed the self-help shelves in my local bookstore. What a life-changer it would prove to be.

I relied heavily on the nine lessons Kelly covers in the book, throughout my recovery and beyond. I followed every step, over and over until they became ingrained in my thinking and my habits.

This book reached out to my heart. To me, it said that it didn't matter where I had been with my depression; all that mattered was where I was heading to now. It was my road map and life raft combined.

Its most critical lesson for me goes like this: "Just do the next right thing." Sounds simple, doesn't it? The secret is that it *was* that simple. And you have no idea how liberating this concept was. We've heard people say, "Just do the next *best* thing." Ah, but doing the next *right* thing is quite a different message. And a very different practice, too. It involves taking a long view, as the author says, as opposed to a short or just-for-now view.

As someone engaged in all-or-nothing thinking at the time, this suggestion told me that it was okay to not be capable of accomplishing the entire thing, whatever that thing happened to be, or for whatever reason—in my case, due to my anxiety and lack of mental energy. Not only did those words make it okay to take on just a tiny piece of the whole—even when I didn't have a clue what the whole might look like—but it felt fantastic to have taken any step at all, however small, in the right direction. That seemingly little concept was huge for me. It was more than good for my mind; it was good for my soul. It offered me a taste of what feeling worthy might be like. Because I had just done something right, hadn't I?!

This lesson helped me to break things down into manageable pieces, which greatly assisted in combating feelings of anxiety and overwhelm; this simple thought, repeated to myself over and over during my day, helped keep my mind focused in the present moment and tuned in to what was important, right now. It helped me to keep worry at bay and reminded me that I could only do what I was able to do in this moment anyway—and that was enough. When I found my mind being drawn to a dark place, those six words—just do the next right thing—helped to kick-start my exit from that "bad" place and move my head into a more neutral space. Speaking those words to myself was like snapping my fingers into gentle action. And for me, taking that small step was often all that was needed to get me out of a funk and into fresh air.

Another groundbreaking notion put forward in Kelly's book is self-discipline. Right away, this idea appealed to me because I had been good at self-discipline once. The author's explanation that discipline can lead to freedom both surprised and appealed to me greatly. I had never come across such an idea before (but I have since), that discipline and freedom can be intertwined. We are more apt to hear the opposite, in fact, that freedom is when you get to do whatever you want whenever you want to do it. But, as Kelly explains, a lack of discipline brings only chaos to a life, not freedom.

I learned that finding the inner strength to apply discipline to any area of my life, at any time, could provide a sense of freedom and power over myself and my thoughts. That felt solid. I immediately brought that notion into my life and started practicing.

The next critical lesson was the importance of developing character. I learned to focus on what was important in life, those things you might wish you had done more of, when looking back from your deathbed. The book taught me how to identify personal virtues and how to amplify ones that needed strengthening in me, as well as how to go about developing new virtues where I felt I was lacking.

I learned what being the best version of myself means and how to achieve that. I accepted that doing my best and being as near to my best self as I could manage is all that anyone can expect of me. And more important, it is all I should expect of myself.

These were powerful concepts that helped me build my self-esteem.

The ninth lesson, for me, was the hardest one to put into practice: "Patiently seek the good in everyone and everything." My natural tendency leans toward being silently critical of others even in the smallest of things. How bad is that! Recently, someone suggested this is a trait common to most humans. Perhaps, but it doesn't excuse the fact. I am still working on reversing this inclination, allowing the positive attributes of people to overtake the others as they float up into my consciousness. Slowly, I am getting closer. I also learned that criticism of others is actually self-criticism in disguise. By adopting this view and addressing those areas in myself, my internal criticism of others has diminished.

> "It is in the quiet of our own hearts that we learn how to calmly manage the present and passionately create the future."
> —Matthew Kelly

Although not at all intended as a guide through depression or anxiety, Kelly's book offered a much-needed structure to help me navigate through a low period in my life, toward a healthier landing place, fully equipped with character, self-discipline (a work in progress), and a realistic assessment of what is possible. It taught me a way out that was clear and easy to follow. Most likely, the draw was so strong for me because I was ripe and ready for the lessons that it offered. And as the book's subtitle suggests, once I reached a state of happiness, I certainly wanted it to be of the enduring kind.

This was arguably the most important book of my recovery. This book was my lifeboat. And it came into my life in the most unexpected and natural of ways. I mentioned previously how delighted I was in finding the perfect journaling book at my local bookstore. I had gone to the store in search of a journal to help kick-start the New Year, but I left with two books in hand. They would turn out to be the written companions that would shape my year and, indeed, the rest of my life.

Perfectly Yourself felt supercharged, and I could imagine Spirit laughing with joy at my catching her lead. It was a perfect example of how Spirit works with us when our awareness is open and tuned in to the right channel. (I highly recommend the practice, because it is such a blast!)

The genius of this book is that not only does it offer a step-by-step process for integrating fundamental changes for making a qualitative difference in your life, but it takes the reader through the psychology of change itself. It illustrates why change most often doesn't last—based on the author's personal experience in dealing with his own struggles, and his knowledge of people collected from more than a decade of speaking engagements to large audiences, and listening to thousands of people share their stories.

I wasn't clear on exactly what changes I needed to make yet, in order to pull myself out of the inevitable patterns of depression, and especially to internalize and normalize the changes in a way that would keep the beast a distant memory—permanently.

I had asked Spirit for guidance and I was blindly following her, with no guarantee mind you, but with a whole lot of faith.

The book helped me to integrate the well-described dynamics of change at a time in my life when major change was called for. I had to learn how to pull myself out of a state of generalized anxiety and a looming depression.

The book taught me what it means to be the best version of myself, the person God had in mind when I was created. It provided a clear and straightforward guidance system for being true to my authentic self, while at the same time, giving of myself in service to others. What more could I ask for?

In the following section, I share some of my favorite learning from *Perfectly Yourself*. I talk about those particular lessons that created lasting change in my life.

Organized in nine chapters—one for each lesson—Kelly conveniently ends each chapter with a set of concrete steps for applying the lesson, in a most practical way. I found myself referencing these pages repeatedly.

CELEBRATE YOUR PROGRESS

I learned to celebrate my progress as a way of reframing my brain's established beliefs about myself (that I would never get better). Step by little step, I proved my brain wrong. I recorded my progress in full, beautiful color in my private blog/journal, where I enjoyed playing with colorful images and funky layouts, as well as in my paper journal and my High-Five book.

Not just my brain needed to be refreshed to the new order but also my mind, my old beliefs, my heart, and my body—the whole of me needed convincing. So I did a lot to mark my progress, as well as the virtues I was growing within me. I wrote in very large, colored letters words that needed repeating and reminding, such as: believe, trust, beauty, mental discipline, creative, successful, joy, perseverance, shine your light, and courage. I pasted these in well-traveled areas in my home, like above the vanity, in my meditation-prayer room, and in my sewing/Joy Room.

Kelly reminds us that, "Life is not about doing and having; it is about becoming... becoming the best-version-of-ourselves. And when we turn our attention to living this dream, our lives are flooded with energy, enthusiasm, passion, purpose, and a real and sustainable joy."

This book opened a path to change for me, and I gladly took the first step. Marking my progress was an important part of that.

When we set our mind to moving forward, we are happiest when we see progress; recognizing progress is a good boost for morale and mood, too.

Just Do the Next Right Thing

The lesson of this chapter saved me more times than I can remember. The idea is that all I needed to do was the one next right thing, not the whole right thing, and not even the best thing, just something *toward* the right thing, however small. I only needed to do the thing that got me closer to a better me. And this small action counted toward my doing something good.

I was able to do that because it asked me to take only a tiny bite. Being able to achieve this small thing during my day was enough to turn the whole day into one of achievement. It amazed me how this worked and how this small thing could have such a positive effect on my overall mental state.

This daily practice led me, over time, to start feeling good about myself. This is no small feat when you are fighting with depression, believe me, at a time when it is much easier and natural to be feeling bad about yourself. It is a genuine uphill battle to be thinking good thoughts in general, and even tougher to be thinking good thoughts about yourself.

Here's an example of me doing the next right thing. We had just finished having every window in our twenty-year-old house replaced by a local company, with which we had dealt previously and were quite pleased. This job took place between Christmas and the New Year, on a very cold and snowy day. It was understandable if the work crew were in a hurry to finish the job and get home for the holidays.

After the workmen had left, I noticed that the grouting around one of the windows was not done properly and looked shoddy. On top of the terrible appearance, I worried about potential long-term effects in terms of providing a proper seal; it certainly would not improve over time. I didn't like what I saw, plus the fact was that the workmanship was not to the company's usual high standard.

I wondered what the owner would say if he could see the work, and I felt that I owed it to him and his good service history to advise him. I decided to visit the shop in person the next day to explain the situation. As expected, he was not pleased to hear about the quality of the work and sent someone that very day to fix it. I don't know if there were any repercussions to my complaint; I hoped the crew would not be chastised, because I could appreciate the challenge of installing windows in the middle of winter.

It would have been easier and certainly more comfortable to let it go and not say anything. I don't like complaining, and I much prefer to make the best of things. But I knew it would have been hard for me to continue recommending the company to others. How unfair I felt this would be to the owner who had always given us the best service and top-quality product, which was manufactured locally. I spoke up as much for him as for us. It was the right thing to do.

Going in to talk to the owner became much easier once I realized it was in the company's best interest. But I wonder if I would have proceeded in the same way had I not been reading Matthew Kelly's book.

Overall, this lesson was a real feather in the cap of my get-well strategy; it did me immeasurable good. I already was practicing CBT thinking to redress my out-of-proportion and black-and-white thinking, flipping catastrophic thoughts into more realistic and less dire ones. But "just do the next right thing" propelled me into action. And there's nothing quite like action to change a person's mood.

I'm glad I learned to listen to my inner voice, the one that is attached to the best version of myself, the one that vibrates with calm and joy and wears a beautiful smile.

Put Character First

I loved this lesson. It helped me to identify what character traits I value, and to work on adopting them as my own, one virtue at a time, step by step. Given my history of depression, my character was filled with battle scars from the struggle over many years, and perhaps I lacked some deep-rooted, honorable character traits. I wanted some of those virtues for myself. I especially value trustworthiness, modesty (of character), authenticity, ageing with dignity, and giving of oneself, and I wanted to develop more of these: kindness, gentleness, patience, and being a good listener.

I began to integrate this lesson into my daily routine.

The first virtue I worked on was kindness. I wanted to be a kinder person so I practiced expressing kindness in little ways with those close to me, and also with neighbors and strangers. I tried to think of them and their needs before my own. I practiced giving of my time (often in small ways, because my priority had to remain on spending most of my time on my get-well plan). I offered to do errands for my husband, I gave small gifts to friends for no particular reason, and I generally practiced paying attention to others. Acts of kindness felt good to do. And being thoughtful and kind boosted my morale.

A second virtue I cultivated was being a good listener. I tried to listen more than talk, to really listen to the speaker's experience of what he or she was saying. I tried not to interrupt people while they spoke. And I found that people told me more things, going into more details.

Another virtue I wanted more of was gentleness. I aspired to be filled with love and tenderness toward others and toward myself. I consciously chose gentle words and shifted my thoughts in that direction.

I practiced patience with myself and, I hope, with others.

Perseverance was another quality I worked on. I certainly had plenty of opportunities to practice this virtue during my time at home.

Most of all, I admired authenticity and humility and I tried to adopt behaviors that supported these traits. I am not sure who said or wrote this, but it captures my heart: "Authenticity trumps perfection." And how!

FIND WHAT YOU LOVE AND DO IT

This was perhaps the easiest principle to incorporate into my life. I love exercising my creative bones with hands-on creations in fabric, yarn, thread, and fiber. I tried to do that as often as I possibly could.

Fiber arts is where I lose all sense of time, where I most enjoy expanding my heart and soul. But my new day job also offered many occasions to grow and give with passion, to connect with engaged and talented colleagues, and together, to build something of value.

Kelly stresses the importance of creating value for yourself through your work, regardless of its nature or stature. There is value to be created in any job when seen with the proper lens.

LIVE WHAT YOU BELIEVE

This translates into aligning our highest values with the actions of daily life. Until I can do that regularly, I don't feel right; I feel that something is off kilter in my world. For example, I mustn't keep truth from people if I value honesty; I mustn't go shopping out of boredom or to avoid being alone if I value reducing consumerism; I must refrain from buying expensive gifts for the neighbors' kids (whom I love dearly) for the same reason and also because I value simplicity; if I value authenticity, I should not pretend that everything is all right when I am not doing well; if I value humility, I must refrain from taking credit when that rightfully belongs to the team as a whole, and I must shine the light on a friend or colleague rather than on me.

This chapter espouses that bringing our actions into alignment with our beliefs will, over time, create a sense of harmony in our lives and within ourselves. It feels wonderful. You can't buy this kind of peace; you can only create it for yourself—with the helping hand of you know who!

BE DISCIPLINED

I love the concept of self-discipline; it always feels so good when you do it, and it produces results. And most important, it gives me a sense of control. Kelly writes that, "to increase the amount of happiness in a given area of your life, increase the amount of discipline—the two are directly linked." I think he is onto something here.

And with self-discipline comes true freedom. This is the basic message of this chapter. The author explains the concept well, and it was a joyful relief to understand how it works. I encountered a similar concept during a weeklong spiritual retreat at my favorite retreat center in Sutton, Québec. It allowed that true freedom can take place in a life that is dedicated to serving God in a disciplined way. Having grown up in the Catholic Church with its numerous rules and regulations, I never would have thought this possible. But I experienced the deep understanding of its truth when I committed my life to serving God and responding to his will, not mine. It became clear to me then what true freedom is: the freeing experience of living in pure joy and happiness, with God as our ultimate boss.

One of my strengths is the ability to focus my complete attention on a project; when an idea grabs me, I am not easily sidetracked. That is, until I have satisfied my curiosity and passion for the topic. Rather than scatter my attention across multiple interesting ideas, I am able to funnel my energy toward a few important ones. During my sabbatical, I dedicated my entire being to learning how to heal and building new habits, especially those of the mind. This took discipline. But because I was very motivated, it didn't feel like hard work, just necessary work.

Daily spiritual connection was key for grounding myself; I created an opportunity each morning for my spirit to plug into the great Source Spirit, so that I would feel supported, understood, and loved for exactly who I was, bumps and all.

SIMPLIFY

This part is about the need to make space in a life for simplicity, for things to evolve as they should, in their own time and place. It's about the need for spending time each and every day in "the classroom of silence," giving God room in my schedule to commune with me, giving me the chance to "hear" him within my heart, giving myself time to discriminate and choose things of value, things that build up my virtues, and letting go of the rest. I learned that if a thing does not build me up into a better version of myself, perhaps it's time for that thing to be gone from my life.

Do we really want to give our precious time to those things that do not nourish the spirit? Can we honestly choose to keep those people or commitments in our lives that suck our energies and leave us feeling depleted or somehow less than our best? Why would we knowingly do that to ourselves? With eyes opened wide, Kelly helps us to distinguish between what contributes to our better self and what takes away from that. You get to choose.

Kelly suggests that we apply discipline to identify our critical success factors in all areas of life: physical, emotional, intellectual, spiritual, work, family, financial, fun, possessions.

Focus on What You Are Here to Give

Because our time on earth is finite (and as I age, this fact becomes even more abundantly clear), I choose to spend that time focused on giving what I am here to give. Not just thinking about it, but making it happen. Observation tells me there is much talking and thinking, but not nearly enough doing and giving.

Kelly underlines the importance of giving of yourself to the world and your community, giving of your skills and talents, your time, your love, your trust, your hope, your goodness, your listening, your support, your understanding, and your compassion. Focus less on what you want or wish to take; that probably will come all by itself without much urging. But giving is something you do with conscious thought and intent. "If we feed and care for our inner life, our outer life will blossom."

The reader is encouraged to live with purpose or mission, mission being defined as "a meeting between self and service," a giving of the best of yourself to meet the needs of others. I support Matthew Kelly in that, at the end of the day, serving is the secret to enjoying enduring happiness.

"Focusing on what we are here to give is one way to build self-esteem." Imagine how good it would feel to provide a service that helps someone to become the best version of herself.

For a quick pick-me-up, I practice making someone's day today, and every day.

Patiently Seek the Good in Everyone and Everything

Perhaps the hardest lesson in the book for me was learning to see the good in everyone. This took some practice, and I still need to remind myself of this lesson from time to time.

This book let me see, accept, and honor my imperfections, "for it is through them that I learn and grow." Knowing that I am meant to be imperfect is a liberating thing. We all are, and I wish you every success in refraining from being anything but kind to yourself. Each of us deserves nothing less.

Focusing on taking one small step at a time toward a better version of myself, not my best self, not yet anyway, by building one piece of my character at a time, I figured that my best self would eventually emerge without further effort. Focusing on improving my character at a time in my life when I felt beneath my usual decent self was an important and therapeutic practice. It gave me back the controls, taking them away from my illness and placing them directly into my own shaky hands.

This book provided a much-needed structure, taught me the core value of discipline, a value I had lost along the way, and how to elevate my character one area at a time, in a solid and lasting way. The process of learning and applying the nine lessons over several months was a liberating and gratifying growth exercise. I was in awe of the insight and intelligence this method offered. It's no wonder that Spirit chose this book to teach me how to regain control of my life. It was precisely what I needed.

• • • EXERCISES • • •

Applying the Deathbed Perspective

- What was this life for?
- What were the most important moments and why?
- To what degree has my life been an expression of my highest truth and understanding?
- Did I consistently do the right thing when it mattered most?
- What are my regrets?

Searching for Purpose

I've come across many people who are searching for meaning in their life, searching for a greater purpose, searching for their mission. This question is often raised during spiritual retreats. And the answer invariably is that people might want to look to their greatest weaknesses or wounds for an answer. I would like to add that if a person can combine his or her weakest areas with a natural talent, then he or she truly has found a healing mission. In my experience, a mission can change or evolve over time, sometimes leading to an expanded mission or to a different one altogether. And we need to agree that this is perfectly fine. Personally, I'm happiest when fulfilling one mission at a time, but that could just be what is most comfortable for me because it suits my temperament best. Others may well lead several missions at once.

I had forgotten the lesson of my grade one teacher—that we are each born with a special talent and that our job on Earth is to develop that talent—until I began working through Sonia Choquette's course. I love the sentiment. It reminds me to be responsible with my God-given talents and not to squander the goodness I have been gifted.

Finding my life's purpose has been a truly gratifying path. And if my mission can help people along the way, then that is the absolute best! To me, that's precisely what life is about in the end—serving the higher good through the joy of expanding our talents. What do you think your purpose or mission might be?

I wanted holistic healing from my battle with depression, generalized anxiety, and PTSD. I needed to learn how to protect myself from those things in life that could cause my illness to flare up and get ugly. Like the Herpes virus (HSV-1) which, once activated by an illness remains latent and preserved in the cells only to be reactivated in the form of a cold sore given the right conditions (a cold, emotional stress, fatigue, or exposure to bright sunlight), my propensity for depression would be a lifelong companion.

Medication helps to stabilize my illness (greatly diminishing the symptoms), but it doesn't protect me from relapse given the "right" circumstances.

I wanted to better understand my mind so I could take appropriate steps to protect it from freaking out when it encountered perceived threats.

Through my desperate call for help in 2010, Spirit guided my education in learning these things. She led me through a methodical, step-by-step healing path that saved my life:

- Through rediscovering creativity and its critical role for my healing

- Through understanding how visualizing my desired outcome helped change my brain and turned those desires into reality
- How establishing a structure for my days and practicing self-discipline gave me confidence in my own abilities
- How reciting positive mantras and rhymes helped to convince my subconscious that I was capable and deserving
- How morning meditation caused my days to unfold just as I had envisioned

I learned how not to let my fears control me and how to take charge of my life and protect myself from having random occurrences turn my world upside down. I gradually learned to trust myself, knowing I was developing the skills to navigate safely in the world, while attempting to keep my sails full.

Best of all, I learned that leading a fulfilling life was a skill that could be learned. And I was determined to learn it.

Following Spirit's footsteps during my year of healing was the most rewarding experience of my life next to raising two fabulous children. (*Caroline et Marcel, je vous aime.*)

ON NEGATIVITY

During my "sabbatical" year, I became an expert at reframing my thoughts to remove any hint of negativity, while making a conscious effort to avoid negative input from external sources like newspapers and TV (especially the news). When it came time to return to work, however, I soon realized that negativity was rampant in that environment (as in most office settings, I expect). If I hoped to survive at work, I needed to find some way of protecting myself from exposure to it, in any form—be it negative space, negative chatter, gossip of any kind, negative people, negative topics, negative conversations, even negative talk about the weather. Anything that hinted of negativity was up for grabs by my vulnerable brain.

I had to avoid it at all costs. Not knowing how to deal with it—other than to run for the hills!—I found it easiest simply to avoid engaging in conversations. And I couldn't care what people might think of my avoidance. Where it was not possible to ignore the negative types, for example, if we were at the same meeting, I would jump over negativity or detour around it. I wore earplugs while working at my computer to avoid hearing it, and I made up excuses to sidestep it. Any and all techniques to circumvent negativity were worth the effort (and lack of attention).

Negativity avoidance became another ingredient in my success-fully-staying-at-work strategy. I was dead serious about it too. No negativity allowed in my space! Naysayers, be gone! After a few years, and as I became more adept at wearing a protective shield while in the workplace, I slowly began to connect with a few positive people, eventually letting down my guard enough to let other "safe" people in, and in time, I was able to be open to everyone. But this took several years of building trust.

I did get bitten by negativity now and again and found myself quite disoriented by it, flustered at not knowing how to cope with it, still being so scared of negativity. I struggled to extricate myself from these people while feeling drawn in to their conversations. That's where my second manager, Liz, was helpful in guiding me. She helped me find harmless detours and worked with me in coming up with plausible excuses that I kept in my back pocket and which allowed me to avoid potentially toxic situations.

Funny enough, Liz had a thing against negativity too; she made the point quite emphatically at our first section meeting. No negativity was allowed within her hearing, only options and solutions. Wow, did I hit the jackpot with this new manager or what?!

> "The more peaceful you become, the easier you can deflect the negative energies of those you encounter. This is like having an invisible shield around you that nothing can penetrate."
> —Wayne Dyer

After an initial bump in our relationship, warranting my explaining the finer points of my needs and limitations, Liz became my greatest ally and support. I might not have made it to retirement without her, certainly not while enjoying such a pleasant final months.

I continue this internal campaign against negativity in my interactions with the world, quite unconsciously by now, as it's become my first response. And I love it. I try to do the same with worry, with mostly satisfactory results. I believe that what we focus on expands, and that "like" attracts its twin, and this helps keep worry in its rightful place—coming out only once in a while, like the good dishes kept for special occasions. I read somewhere that ninety-five percent of what we worry about never happens anyway. I find it sad to imagine all the grief and wasted effort over some imaginary problem. Maybe it's worth figuring out a way to avoid worry at all and focus our energy on making good things happen instead.

MAKING FRIENDS

Remember when worrying about having to make new friends as you headed off to grade one or a new school, and you shared your concern with your mom or dad, and he or she said, "Well, just smile and say hello first, and introduce yourself." Did that work for you? Naw, me neither. I was way too shy or nervous to make the first move. And besides, the kids always teased me because of my red hair. I was sure they would never like me because of it, even though my mom said that they wouldn't bother teasing me if they didn't like me. I didn't buy it at the time because it made me feel so sad, but there might be some truth to it. At least they noticed me!

After my first big depression, I realized that having no friends was not healthy for me—not healthy for anyone, but especially not for someone with depressive tendencies. I decided I needed to change that circumstance and work on making good friends. I had acquaintances, but I needed more.

Growing up, this introvert was happy having just one best friend at a time. And because my family moved a lot—every move taking us to slightly improved living quarters sometimes in a better neighborhood—it meant I changed schools often, which naturally involved making new friends. You would think that with all that early training I would have learned how to make friends quickly. Instead, I learned to be self-contained and satis-fied with entertaining myself. Growing up in a large family, my sisters were stand-ins for good friends. I told myself that I didn't need friends, that friends only brought problems anyhow. And I found that I had little in common with the people I met socially. I was fine on my own. And for the most part, I did okay, until depression took control of my life and taught me that social-izing was important, and that I needed people in my life.

After I recovered and was well again, I felt ready and open to making friends. I tried being friendly with the neighbors, two very nice ladies who lived on our road and attended the local Pentecostal church. One of them invited me to a service, but after a few tries, I found it was not a good fit for me. I joined the Roman Catholic Church but found no friends there—ours being a small village, the women already knew each other, and after half a dozen Sundays of feeling alone, I switched to another, larger church in the nearby city. Bad move, because all the women there were from a different community, and as a result, there were few occasions to interact. I joined an exercise class in the village and a scrapbooking group. On and on my efforts went, still with no new friends.

In 2007, I decided to spend two months volunteering in Peru. I was seeing a therapist for my migraines as I prepared to leave the country. I had heard good things about EFT (Emotion Freedom Technique) as a practice for eliminating physical pain, and my therapist used this technique among others. On my last visit, having done what we could regarding the migraines, she asked if there was anything else that I wished to put out to the universe for assistance. I explained that I wanted to make some friends, and as is part of the practice, she asked me to get specific in my desire. I told her what I was hoping for, which she relayed out loud to the universe. I wanted to find a woman with similar interests, who enjoyed handcrafts like knitting and sewing, and exploring spirituality, someone who would become a very good friend. I let that desire float as I packed my bags for my South American solo adventure.

While in Peru, I was amazed at how easily and naturally I was able to make friends with locals and the other volunteers. It was fun and I was living in joy! I didn't feel self-conscious or nervous when approaching new people, most of whom were decades younger. I was being my truest self and people responded to me! When I told this to my husband on our weekly telephone dates, he too was surprised, and happy for me.

A few weeks following my return to work, I got a call from a colleague who worked in a different department and who was looking for help with her knitting. Her name was Sue and I had met her when working on a project together, but I didn't know anything about her. We met in the cafeteria to look at her knitting question and we ended up talking feverishly for more than an hour. We had so much in common. She was just getting back to knitting after a twenty-year hiatus; she once had a sewing business making antique-looking dolls; and she knew first-hand about living with depression. I suspected that Spirit had brought us together, especially when Sue relayed how nervous she had been in approaching me for knitting advice, and how being that forward and phoning me out of the blue was quite out of character. She felt something had pushed her to do it.

We have been close friends ever since. We've been through a lot together and she reinforces for me the notion that friends not only can be fun, but are necessary for good health.

A few days after our first gab session over knitting, I remember thinking that the universe was working on bringing me a friend just like I asked, and I wondered if that friend might be Sue or possibly Heather, another colleague I liked a lot, also from a different department. Though it took a little longer to develop, Heather also has become a very dear friend to me.

A few years after my encounter with Sue, I decided I could handle having another friend. I felt that three was a very good number and I was ready to spread my wings a bit. Naturally, I told Spirit about my desire. Along would come Carol B., my third awesome friend indeed.

It was decided that my work unit of three would be relocated to the Human Resources branch. Guess where Carol worked? A stranger to me at the time, she welcomed me into her section literally with open arms—giving me the best hug ever—and as we got to know each other, she made me feel wanted and smart and talented at a time when I desperately needed the boost. We didn't become instant friends outside of work—that happened after she retired—but I knew she was the third person I had asked for. I just did! I wrote about her in my journal: "May 16, 2011, Today, I made a new friend. Her name is Carol." She retired in 2013.

> "Without inspiration the best powers of the mind remain dormant; there is a fuel in us which needs to be ignited with sparks."
> —Johann Gottfried von Herder

Sue, Heather, and Carol were the three friends, along with my Peterborough family, who helped me celebrate my signing a book deal, which is one of the most important things to have happened in my life.

The next time depression hit, I had friends to call on for support. Recovery was a healthier experience for me because I could share my struggles with friends who understood, cared, and listened. Along with my family, they prayed for me to get better. And I am able to support them in a similar way. It feels right and very good to have friends.

● ● ● EXERCISE ● ● ●

Raising Your Positives: Five Things for Better Health
This wisdom is from Master Chunyi Lin, Spring Forest Qigong.
Do this daily as a way to ground yourself:

1. S.M.I.L.E. (Start My Internal Love Engine)
2. Slow breathing and low chanting (fifteen minutes)
3. Connect to your spiritual Source and speak the connection mantra-style, "I connect to the Source"
4. Visualize the Source energy sending golden light into your heart
5. Allow yourself to be a love radiator—the more positive energy you send, so you will receive

MY HIGH-FIVE BOOK

I kept track of any compliment and positive word that came my way, no matter how insignificant the sentiment appeared. Having these comments written down was proof of my competence at something, anything.

This was an important step for building my self-esteem. What I might once have judged to be a practice for the self-absorbed, I now understood was an important step for my getting well. I needed to convince my brain of what others seemed to know.

Writing every good thing that others said about me, however small, did feel silly at first until I noticed that my spirit began to lift. I noticed the smile on my face each time I added a new entry to the book. I started believing what I wrote, that I was not a worthless person after all, and that if someone out there considered me of value, perhaps I should too.

DECEMBER 2011—A TELLING ENTRY

After a particularly difficult day at the office, where I became splattered with nasty people's workplace toxins, it was important to reframe my thoughts and put the flow right again. I placed a sticker in the center of a page with a quote by Eleanor Roosevelt: "No one can make you feel inferior without your consent." And using bright crayons in yellow, red, green, and blue, I colored rays like a sunny force field emanating from all sides of the small sticker, reaching the outer edges of the page, filling it with vibrant colors and energy.

I knew I held the power to change my mood by switching my thoughts.

I wish I could give credit to the author of the High-Five book idea but I don't recall where I got it from; please forgive my lapse.

Here is a sampling my other entries.

December 8, 2010
My manager told me our director and assistant deputy minister did not change a thing on my work (three promotional pieces I wrote for our website's "Spotlight on Engagement" series). He was quite surprised by that because, evidently, executives are prone to making changes to anything and everything that comes across their desks for approval. Good for me!! Only my second week back on the job and my value is already being recognized. That does feel good, and I'm glad he told me.

January 17, 2011
From my colleague who was the content expert for the participant manual I created, which was my first project following my return to work in 2010.

"She is so proud of the product I developed that she says she wants a signed copy! Ha-ha! She says I have really raised the bar now for all training manuals. And that it is the best she has ever seen in her thirty years in the learning and development business. How's that for a high-five!"

Following the launch and orientation session of the initiative for which the manual was developed, and which I helped to design as well as manage the audio-visual component remotely:

"The deputy is super pleased! And the chief officer said: This was one of the tightest and smoothest orientation sessions she has attended. And she has attended twenty-two!"

March 2–3 weekend, 2012
This entry is in reference to a daylong meditation and prayer session that I facilitated, workshop-style, for my sister Lorraine during an especially difficult time in her life.

"I feel better; this workshop really helped. I feel calmer. I feel that I'm okay, not scared anymore of handling this house while my husband is away... I don't have the fear that I did before. You really helped me; this is exactly what I needed.

"When we held hands and you were praying for guidance, I could feel the comfort and soothing in your hands. You have beautiful hands, strong and capable, like Mom's. There is real strength there, and I could feel that so clearly! You would make an excellent life coach." (Gee, thanks a bunch, sis.)

Knowing that my life is at stake is a thought that continues to hover at the back of my mind, helping to inform my daily choices.

In January 2014, I experienced some early-warning signals of an imminent potential depression "event." But because I treated these invisible signs as emergencies—which they were—and initiated immediate intervention, I was able to remain at my job throughout the shaky process.

I worked with my manager on adjusting my work to fit my immediate needs (taking on simpler tasks that my brain felt safe doing) and gradually adjusting the work up to my usual level over several weeks as my condition improved.

For me, that is true success! It's about learning to live *with* a mental illness and working through issues as they arise while remaining a productive and well person. We learn to make adjustments for physical illnesses or limitations, don't we? We learn to use crutches when nursing a broken ankle, to use voice-recognition computer software if our hands lose their mobility, to change our diet in response to high blood pressure.

We need to learn to treat mental illness with the same attention and respect.

I experienced a second flare-up later that year when I got a new boss due to my manager's retirement. The incoming manager was fairly new to our branch and knew me only in passing. While she had been briefed on my medical circumstances and workplace accommodation (by my manager alone as well as with the three of us together), it turned out she didn't fully understand how things needed to be in order for me to remain healthy at work.

Once my manager retired, my work-related stress started to build, as did some familiar early signs of trouble; I needed to halt the regression immediately.

"Women are like teabags; we don't know our true strength until we are in hot water!"
—Eleanor Roosevelt

I decided to take charge of the situation by calling a meeting with my new manager, Liz, to explain my concerns. And because I was feeling quite vulnerable by this point, I invited a colleague, whom I'll call Joanne, who was respected by both my boss and me, to sit in as my support. I assured her she wouldn't need to say anything, just be there in case I needed her. Having Joanne there made me feel safe.

Being prepared to escalate the issue, should my manager not be receptive to my concerns, prevented me from feeling trapped and helpless. Because I had a plan.

I came to the meeting with my issues written down, which I began to read out loud. (I couldn't trust my brain to remember what I wanted to say, or to have the nerve to say all I needed to say.) I explained why Liz's response to a particular and ongoing circumstance was unacceptable, that it contributed to my backsliding and why. I also explained what I needed from her instead.

Liz reacted with such grace and acceptance that it floored me. I was ready for battle but was grateful for the peace. The meeting went better than I could have hoped for. She acknowledged my concerns and apologized for her earlier response. We agreed to put the situation behind us and to start fresh.

From then on, Liz was like a different person toward me, hugely supportive and understanding, always with an encouraging word and an open door should I ever need her help or support. Liz turned out to be the best manager I could have dreamed of. I appreciate her beyond words, and I also like her a lot.

I accept that it is my job to educate the people around me about my needs and limitations. How could I hope for my manager to understand and to provide for my workplace needs, to know what I can and cannot do, if I don't give her that information? Sure, my doctor can answer written questions and give a medical prognosis, but I am the expert on what works best for me in the day-to-day.

Along the path to becoming well, I have had to reinvent myself not only to survive but to *thrive* and contribute in a way that works for me.

I came to realize that I would always have a mental illness and I taught myself how to live with that condition. Like losing a non-functioning limb, I may have lost my old self, but I have gained so much more because of the illness; it made me see who I truly am and gave me a genuine, strong voice. How could I not be grateful for that?

My illness forced me to grow in places that I did not have the courage to face before. Not that I was given a choice. In life, we are sometimes not given a choice. But we can choose how we respond, whether we allow ourselves to be permanently crushed or to be renewed like a phoenix rising from the ashes.

I took up the challenge and learned new practices that helped me become a stronger person—because my life was at stake.

Early Intervention Can Lead to Prevention

Understanding my triggers was critical, and learning to recognize them early was key, because it is easier to prevent the triggers than to diffuse them once they have been activated. Once activated, whatever triggered the response (anxiety and depression) is almost beside the fact at that point. By then, you are having to manage the illness back down, and that takes way more effort and involves mental and emotional pain and anguish. Like any medical emergency, the sooner treatment can begin, the better the chances for a fruitful recovery. Now you see the genius of focusing your attention on preventing triggers and arresting whatever is aggravating the triggerpoint. For me, this approach has been very productive; it meant that I could take the controls back and manage the illness my way.

It takes being bold—in sticking to my resolve and listening to my inner voice, at the risk of appearing selfish or some other derogatory label. I learned to love my inner voice dearly and I respect her for her wisdom and sense of timing. I must not care about what people might think regarding my lack of contact, even when they tell me that they miss me. I'm sorry, but I don't believe in guilt. Because I know very deeply that if I don't ensure that I get the things I need to be well, who else will? Who else can?

I developed some "sacred" rules to support my well-being:

1. I limit my exposure to groups (like office lunches, retirements, and family gatherings).
2. I make time for solitude every day.
3. I schedule recovery days midweek and following a weekend away from home.
4. I recognize the need for balance in all aspects of my life and try to maintain moderation in all things. Let me tell you, this is not easy for someone with an intense personality; it takes constant reminding.
5. I ensure that creativity holds a central place of my world, reserving time to playfully make things in my sewing room.
6. I insist on getting plenty of sleep; I become emotionally fragile when I am tired or overstimulated (just like a baby or young child).
7. I eat good, home-cooked food, and I don't skip meals.

I am not responsible for my disability. But I *am* responsible for teaching people how to treat me. When I behave with confidence, I am showing others how to behave toward me.

REMISSION: WHAT DOES THAT LOOK LIKE?

I choose to use the word *remission* versus recovery because by now, depression is a lifelong illness for me, and I probably will be on medication for the rest of my life—thank goodness! Though the symptoms are not always evident—I experienced four years of remission without even a hiccup—the dangers are always there, waiting for me to let my guard down.

I've learned to jealously protect my well-being like a mother bear guards her cub. Because my life is at stake.

Had it not been for my employer's process for workplace accommodation, I would not have been capable of finishing my employment until retirement. My job responsibilities and hours of work were adjusted to directly support me in my needs and capabilities. The arrangement was absolutely central to my well-being and it greatly contributed to my success as a mental illness survivor.

She's Back, But Is She Normal?

When I returned to work after my initial yearlong absence in 2002, I could almost hear the reaction from colleagues: "So, she's back! But is she normal?" I have always been open about my illness and its effects; I have nothing to hide and I don't believe in furthering the stigma that depression carries. I figured, "How else are people going to learn about what I can and cannot do?"

On a later attempt to reintegrate the workplace, following a six-month absence, I had been assigned a project by my director, whom I knew, but not well. We met in his office and the first thing he told me was: "Michèle, I'm going to treat you the same as I always have. Because for me, nothing has changed."

> "The opposite of depression is not happiness, but vitality."
> —Andrew Solomon

I believe he meant to reassure me that he held no judgment as a result of my having been away on "stress leave." Instead, the statement had the opposite effect; it created a sense of panic in me. *Oh no*, I thought, *I'm in real trouble if he thinks I can be the same as before and perform to the same level!*

I remained silent while he explained what the project he had in mind entailed. I was to form a team to organize the next staff day, an event involving people from three locations across the province. He was looking for something unique to pull people together, and he thought I would be perfect for the job. He would suggest some people I could ask to sit on the team and work with me.

I left his office frozen in fear. I couldn't do what he asked! I couldn't approach people and lead a team. I couldn't even talk to these people, let alone be engaging and upbeat! I couldn't access my creative mind. I was in trouble here. He would think I was lazy, or unmotivated, or that I didn't care. What could I do? Panic.

When I reached my desk, I put that project aside for the moment and picked up another task, something more straightforward. I was to summarize handwritten notes from a colleague who had led a group brainstorming session the previous week. But I couldn't do it. My brain could not think or interpret the information. The phrases made no sense; they didn't connect to one another. I knew the meaning of the words, but I could not link them to the whole, what phrases went with which idea. That's when I knew that I was not ready to return to work.

Regrettably, the panic I felt from meeting with my director caused my brain to freeze and my symptoms to relapse worse than before. I was back on leave, where I remained a further six months.

Lesson learned: Do not be a hero and return to work prematurely.

When I am doing well, I can understand if those around me forget that I have a disability, because I look and sound fine. It's invisible, after all. Heck, I sometimes forget it myself! But I am not able to take on a "normal" load, not at work or at home.

Not even when it's for something fun. I know that if I go away for the weekend, I will need to book Monday off as a vacation day to recover and recharge. I know that I need a recovery day midweek, so that I can be productive on the four days that I am at work.

Thanks to a wise human resources consultant, my reintegration into the workplace was successful through a work-hardening program. I spent six months doing progressively more responsible duties. I started with the simplest of tasks, entering personnel data into a computer and I slowly advanced through other tasks to eventually editing correspondence.

I was able to return to my home position six months later almost to the day, with some job modifications. Clearly, someone knew something about how people heal, that it would take six months exactly for me to become proficient again and able to do the type of work I did before the illness. My job had been redesigned during my absence, for the better I might add, and I was glad to now report to an experienced and skilled manager, which the job had previously sadly lacked.

To think that I had previously offered to give my job away to someone more qualified, so convinced was I that I could never go back to doing the same kind of work. But the wise HR person insisted that my job be protected and held for me the full six months to which I was entitled. She clearly knew enough about how quickly things can change when dealing with mental health issues.

SMALLER BATTERY AND LIMITED CAPACITY FOR STRESS

My illness means that I have a smaller personal battery that needs more frequent recharging. I have a low tolerance for stress of any kind, which, if not properly monitored, can threaten my ability to cope and potentially to relapse.

A few years ago, my husband had a surgical procedure. Hospitals being what they are these days, he was released the next day. Soon after, he developed a complication that meant having to return to the hospital and wait hours in the emergency department, only to be told that everything was progressing as expected and there was nothing to worry about. Except a whole lot of stress.

I had booked the week off to look after him, and since his mobility was limited, I was kept busy all day and evening looking after the necessities and going up and down stairs. On the fifth day, I realized I could not keep up the pace any longer; I had reached my limit. I knew I was nearing exhaustion—the uncontrollable tears being the final signal. I needed to rest.

I was experiencing telltale signs of overload and I had to look after myself if I hoped to prevent further deterioration. It would do us no good if we were both ill. I immediately made arrangements to stay with a friend for a few days. And I made other arrangements for a family member to check in with Robert over the weekend. After clearing the plan with the visiting nurse practitioner, I was off for a much-needed respite.

When I returned home three days later, feeling refreshed and in a much better place mentally and emotionally, Robert and I discussed what had happened. Due to the mental stress, I had been unable to explain what was happening to me at the time, and why I needed to leave when I did. I also did not want to add my own worries to his health burden. We agreed that in the future, should either of us find ourselves in a similar position of need, we would make prior arrangements for home care and ensure that I was properly supported.

Having the caregiver become sick is a classic situation that can be prevented with proper awareness and planning.

It is important that I be self-aware without being self-indulgent—another balancing act.

Being an essentially pragmatic person, I've put the bleak stuff behind me, and rarely do I look upon it. Writing this book has lead me to reexamine my path over the last fourteen years; the process has been both challenging and rewarding, especially if my story can inspire someone who is struggling right now.

During some of those years, I did feel some guilt at having to rely on my work colleagues more than I once did and more than I ever wanted to, being an independent and self-sufficient person by nature.

I have felt unworthy and sub-par, and my work-image took a hard beating (from my perspective, anyway).

In the earlier years of my illness, I felt anger at my employer (a faceless organization) for allowing a job to get so big and be given so few resources as to cause someone's emotional break-down. Their not acknowledging any responsibility for that was hard to accept. Thankfully, I have let go of that anger, because it wasn't serving me at all.

I felt grief for the pain I had suffered in the darkest times, when I could not function in the world. And I mourned the years that were lost to the illness.

But I am free of those emotions now.

I had to learn through trial and error what work I could and could not do, and admit that leading ministry-wide initiatives and juggling many responsibilities at once was the quickest way to send me over the edge. On the other hand, I could really flourish by incorporating creativity into my work.

"Nothing will ever be attempted if all possible objections must first be overcome."

—Samuel Johnson

Through a number of false starts (some with severe consequences), I have learned that the only person I must answer to is myself, in partnership with Higher Spirit.

Today, with more than a dozen years of experience at managing my illness, I rarely give in to the inner guilt talk or to second-guessing myself, or to what I imagine others must be thinking about me, or attempting to meet their expectations. I say rarely, because I still catch myself doing it now and then. And when I do, I know exactly what steps to take to neutralize that thought process and quickly get back to a healthier place.

I have become adept at differentiating between the voice of ego and that of my authentic self. Ego wants to please and be "a good girl," and my truest self wants to look after my best interests, to keep me safe.

I know I have disappointed some people over the years, but I just can't do it their way. Because my life is at stake. How can others begin to understand my needs and how I must manage my world in order to stay healthy? How can they see that if I do that thing according to their wishes, it could cost me dearly from my mental health account? So I don't even try to explain myself anymore; I just do what I need to and pay little attention to perceptions. I have learned how to control my own thoughts, but I'm not skilled in controlling theirs. And it is not my job, anyway.

ACKNOWLEDGMENTS

• Robert—My loving husband whom I trust with my life.

• Sue—My dearest friend, who has always been there for me, asking for nothing in return, and needing no explanations.

• Dr. DVL—M.D., family practitioner, who has seen me through the highs and lows over twenty years as my primary physician.

• Dr. PW—M.D., general practitioner specializing in treating depression and anxiety, who taught me to be gentle with myself, how to practice Cognitive Behavior Therapy, and how to change my expectations.

• Dr. UU—Ph.D., homoeopathic doctor and acupuncturist, a truly empathetic woman.

• Dr. BP—Chiropractor extraordinaire, for your calming strength.

• SM—Massage therapist, muscle whisperer, and generous provider.

• RE—My team lead, now retired, the best colleague and greatest support during some personally difficult years. Thank you for seeing through the muck to the brilliance.

• JV—Now retired, an experienced manager who understood her role as a partner in supporting me in the workplace. Thank you for being the solid support at a time when I needed it most.

• CLM—Manager extraordinaire, who knows just what to say to help me turn things around for myself and land facing up. Thank you for managing with style!

• DY—My dear, first-great-manager, when I needed your solid, unhurried support at a vulnerable time in my life. Thank you.

- To my "believing eyes," I love you for knowing I could succeed even when I didn't see it: Lorraine (aka Zoz), Anne, Elvira, Sue, Carol, Heather, and EM.
- Caroline and Marcel, my precious children, for being your truest selves.
- Andy, I appreciate your kind heart and thoughtfulness.
- *Ma chère maman,* for being a model of strength and *débrouillardise. Je t'aime!*
- And finally, a huge thank you to my publisher, KiCam Projects, especially Jennifer and Lori, for trusting that I could carry this story, and Katie, for guiding me to the optimal structure for the tale. Jennifer, there is no way I could do this without your support. You are an angel.

RECORD OF MY DEPRESSION EVENTS

2002: Deep clinical depression—eleven months on medical leave; premature return to work after five months caused relapse for a further six months; eventually returned to the same job following a very gradual work-hardening process over a six-month period.

2005: Five months on medical leave—"event" driven by fear and not knowing how to manage the illness; returned to same job without job-hardening (the opportunity was not presented to me).

2009-2010: Twelve months on medical leave—additional diagnoses: generalized anxiety and post-traumatic stress disorder (PTSD). My "sabbatical" year and the setting for this book.

2014 and 2015: Early-alarm signals detected on three occasions; medical leaves were not needed due to early intervention.

Along with those in the bibliography, I've compiled some resources here that may help you on your journey.

Choquette, Sonia. "Creating Your Heart's Desire," self-paced course with thirty video sessions laid out in nine principles, or weeks, www.soniachoquette.com/hearts-desire.html.

Hamilton, Craig. "Integral Enlightenment—Evolving Beyond Ego," an online course.

Hicks, Esther and Jerry. *Ask and It Is Given*. Carlsbad, CA: Hay House, 2004. The International Focusing Institute, www.focusing.org.

Mental Health and Work: Impact, Issues and Good Practices, World Health Organization, www.who.int/mental_health/meda/en/712.pdf.

Moods Magazine, online Canadian magazine on mental illness, www.moodsmag.com.

NoStigmas.org, mental health network.

Rain, Mary Summer, and Alex Greystone. *Mary Summer Rain's Guide to Dream Symbols*. Newburyport, MA: Hampton Roads, 1996.

SickNotWeak.com, online mental health community.

These are some of the books that helped me to understand what was happening to me, and taught me how to cope, to heal, and later, to thrive. You might find them helpful, too.

Burns, Dr. David D. *Feeling Good: The New Mood Therapy.* New York: Avon, 1992.

Dyer, Wayne. *Living the Wisdom of the TAO: The Complete Tao Te Ching and Affirmations.* Carlsbad, CA: Hay House, 2008.

_____. *10 Secrets for Success and Inner Peace.* Carlsbad, CA: Hay House, 2001.

Gafni, Marc. *Soul Prints: Your Path to Fulfillment.* New York: Pocket, 2001.

Gendlin, Eugene T., Ph.D. *Focusing.* New York: Bantam, 1982.

Harpur, Tom. *Finding the Still Point: A Spirituality Response to Stress.* Kelowna, British Columbia: Northstone, 2005.

Kabat-Zinn, Jon. *Wherever You Go There You Are: Mindfulness Meditation in Everyday Life.* New York: Hyperion, 1994.

Kelly, Matthew. *Perfectly Yourself.* North Palm Beach, Fla.: Beacon Publishing, 2006.

Meattie, Melody. *Finding Your Way Home: A Soul Survival Kit.* New York: Harper Collins, 1998.

Pennington, M. Basil OCSO, *Centered Living: The Way of Centering Prayer.* Liguori, MO: Liguori, 1999.

Rufus, Anneli. *Party of One: The Loners' Manifesto.* Boston, MA: Da Capo, 2003.

Tolle, Eckhart. *A New Earth: Awakening to Your Life's Purpose.* New York: Penguin, 2006.

ABOUT THE AUTHOR
Michèle Swiderski is a creative. When not weaving, spinning, sewing, or knitting, she enjoys connecting with nature at her cabin in the woods. Over the past 15 years, Michèle has struggled with depression and feels she is a better person for it. Recently retired from a career in public service, she is dedicated to raising awareness for mental health and shares her insights on her blog at micheleswiderski.com.